THE GREAT WHITE SHARK

By Sara Green

BELLWETHER MEDIA • MINNEAPOLIS, MN

Jump into the cockpit and take flight with Pilot books. Your journey will take you on high-energy adventures as you learn about all that is wild, weird, fascinating, and fun!

This edition first published in 2013 by Bellwether Media, Inc.

No part of this publication may be reproduced in whole or in part without written permission of the publisher. For information regarding permission, write to Bellwether Media, Inc., Attention: Permissions Department, 5357 Penn Avenue South, Minneapolis, MN 55419.

Library of Congress Cataloging-in-Publication Data

Green, Sara, 1964-
The great white shark / by Sara Green.
  p. cm. – (Pilot books: shark fact files)
Includes bibliographical references and index.
Summary: "Engaging images accompany information about the great white shark. The combination of high-interest subject matter and narrative text is intended for students in grades 3 through 7"–Provided by publisher.
ISBN 978-1-60014-803-3 (hardcover : alk. paper)
1. White shark–Juvenile literature. I. Title.
QL638.95.L3G76 2013
597.3'3–dc23

                    2011053021

TABLE OF CONTENTS

GREAT WHITE SHARK
IDENTIFIED

Beneath the surface of the ocean swims a fearsome predator. Its body is shaped like a torpedo. It has powerful jaws and a pointed snout. Its large, triangular dorsal fin slices through the water. This is the great white shark, the largest predatory fish in the ocean!

The shark swims near an island and catches the scent of seals, its favorite prey. It lifts its head out of the water and spots them swimming nearby. The shark moves quietly under a seal. With tremendous speed, the great white swims upward. It rams into the seal and bites it with razor-sharp teeth. It quickly devours the surprised seal. Now full, the shark can wait several weeks before it must hunt again.

The great white shark's scientific name is *Carcharodon carcharias.* It comes from the Greek words *carcharos*, meaning "ragged," and *odon*, meaning "tooth."

The great white shark gets its name from its white belly. Its back is bluish gray. This countershading helps the shark catch prey by surprise. Fish looking down at a great white see only dark ocean water. Fish looking up see only light from the surface.

The great white's body is covered with flat, pointed scales called dermal denticles. These scales are packed together tightly. They protect the great white from injury and help it move smoothly through water.

The great white can grow to be 21 feet (6.4 meters) long, but it averages between 12 and 16 feet (3.7 and 4.9 meters). Adult females are generally larger than males. The largest great whites can weigh up to 5,000 pounds (2,270 kilograms).

great white shark

human

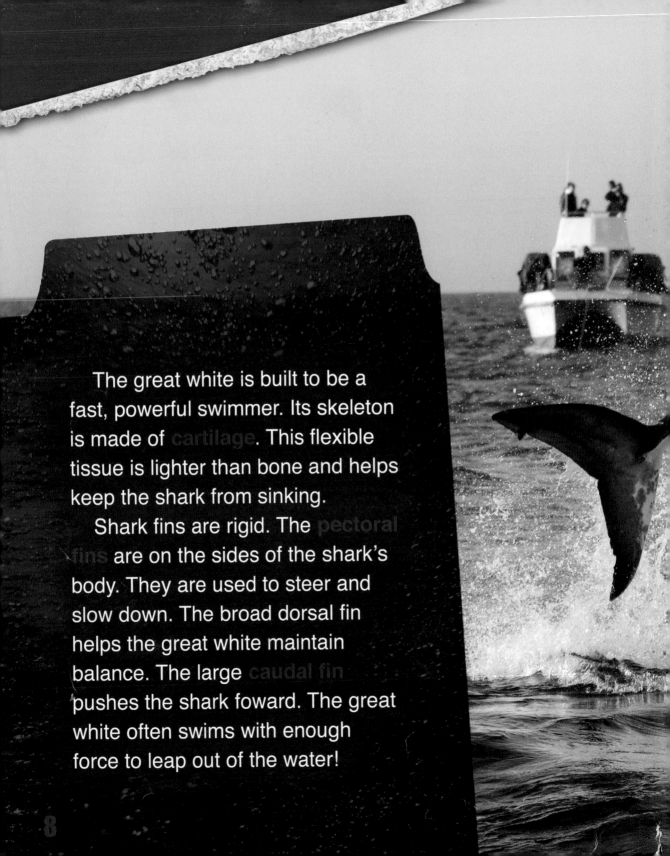

The great white is built to be a fast, powerful swimmer. Its skeleton is made of cartilage. This flexible tissue is lighter than bone and helps keep the shark from sinking.

Shark fins are rigid. The pectoral fins are on the sides of the shark's body. They are used to steer and slow down. The broad dorsal fin helps the great white maintain balance. The large caudal fin pushes the shark foward. The great white often swims with enough force to leap out of the water!

FEEL THE BURN

Great white sharks can increase their body temperatures to be warmer than the surrounding water. Very few fish can do this. Warmer muscles boost the shark's energy and speed.

GREAT WHITE SHARK TRACKED

Great whites are usually found along coastlines in temperate oceans. They like to hunt for prey near islands, especially those inhabited by seals and sea lions. Great whites also swim in the deep waters of the open ocean. They have been spotted in waters as shallow as 3 feet (1 meter) and as deep as 4,200 feet (1,280 meters).

Many great whites migrate across the oceans every year. They travel to warmer waters in the winter to follow prey and give birth to young. Researchers are able to track great whites as they travel. They attach an electronic tag to a great white's dorsal fin. The tag records information about the shark's migration patterns. Researchers now know that many great whites travel to the same places every year.

= great white shark territory

The female great white is ovoviviparous. Eggs hatch inside her body. The pups feed on unhatched eggs and smaller pups in the uterus. About one year later, the mother gives birth to a litter of two to ten pups. They can be up to 5 feet (1.5 meters) long. The pups are born with a full set of teeth and are ready to hunt. They swim away from their mother immediately after birth. She might eat them if they hang around!

Male great whites mature when they are around 10 years old. Females mature several years later. Great whites live and hunt alone for most of their lives. Many researchers believe they live up to 30 years, but some think great whites can live for 60 years or longer.

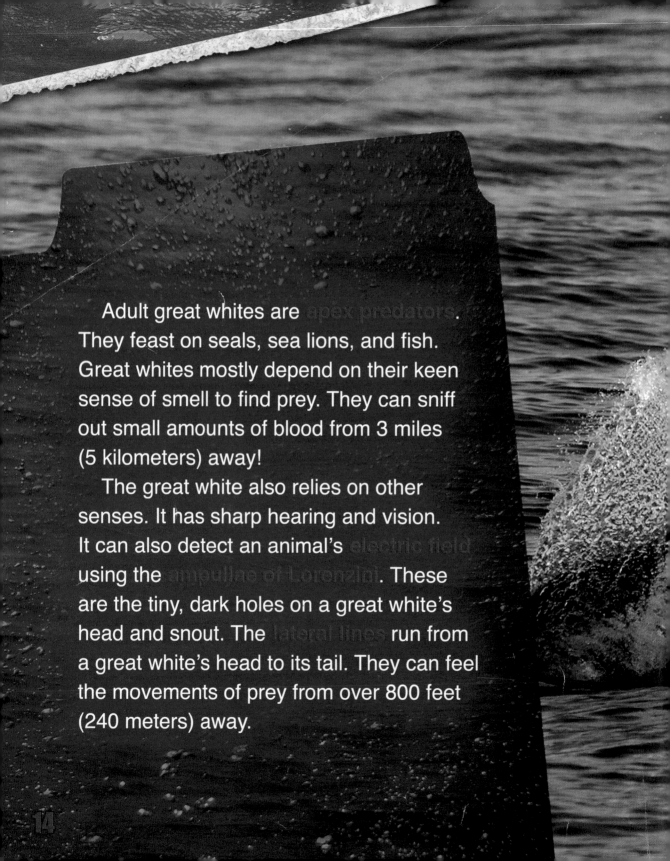

Adult great whites are apex predators. They feast on seals, sea lions, and fish. Great whites mostly depend on their keen sense of smell to find prey. They can sniff out small amounts of blood from 3 miles (5 kilometers) away!

The great white also relies on other senses. It has sharp hearing and vision. It can also detect an animal's electric field using the ampullae of Lorenzini. These are the tiny, dark holes on a great white's head and snout. The lateral lines run from a great white's head to its tail. They can feel the movements of prey from over 800 feet (240 meters) away.

SPEED DEMON

Adult great whites can reach speeds of up to 35 miles (56 kilometers) per hour. However, they can only maintain these speeds for a short time.

The great white has several rows of serrated teeth. The triangular teeth can be up to 3 inches (7.6 centimeters) long. They can slice easily through the skin, muscles, and bones of prey. The first two rows are used to capture and eat prey. When these teeth break, wear down, or fall out, teeth from the back rows move forward to replace them.

Great whites do not eat people, but they will attack them. They are responsible for 5 to 10 attacks every year. This is more than any other kind of shark. Researchers think great whites mistake people for seals. Once a great white realizes it has bitten a human, it usually lets go and swims away. Still, a single bite can be deadly.

BIG GULP

The great white shark does not chew its food. It rips prey into smaller pieces that it swallows whole. A great white shark can eat a 400-pound (180-kilogram) seal in about ten bites.

Great whites are important to all ocean life. They keep prey populations from growing too large. They eat sick, weak, and slow prey. The stronger prey survive to give birth to healthier young. Great whites also keep the oceans clean by eating dead whales, seals, and sharks.

Some researchers believe that fewer than 5,000 great whites remain in the wild. The sharks are caught for their fins, jaws, and teeth. Many also die when they get tangled in fishing nets. The United States and other countries have agreed to ban the trade of items made from great whites. They have also passed laws that protect great whites from fishing nets and hunting. Currently, the great white shark is classified as vulnerable by the International Union for Conservation of Nature (IUCN).

19

SHARK BRIEF

Common Name: Great White Shark

Also Known As: Great White, White Shark, White Pointer

Nickname: White Death

Claim to Fame: Most attacks on humans

Hot Spots: Eastern and Western United States
Hawaii
Western South America
Mediterranean Sea
Japan
Eastern China
South Africa
Australia
New Zealand

Life Span: 30 years or more

Current Status: Vulnerable (IUCN)

EXTINCT

EXTINCT IN THE WILD

CRITICALLY ENDANGERED

ENDANGERED

VULNERABLE

NEAR THREATENED

LEAST CONCERN

Great whites are a thrill to see in their natural habitat. Most people try to spot great whites from boats. Some adventurous divers enjoy the excitement of being in the water with the large predators. They stay safe in special cages that can withstand an attack.

Many scientists fear great whites will not survive into the next century. The sharks mature slowly and do not reproduce often. Their numbers shrink quickly when they are overhunted. It is up to the combined efforts of researchers, lawmakers, and everyday people to save this deadly marvel of nature.

GLOSSARY

ampullae of Lorenzini—a network of tiny jelly-filled sacs around a shark's snout; the jelly is sensitive to the electric fields of nearby prey.

apex predators—predators that are not hunted by any other animal

cartilage—firm, flexible connective tissue that makes up a shark's skeleton

caudal fin—the tail fin of a fish

countershading—coloring that helps camouflage an animal; fish with countershading have pale bellies and dark backs.

dermal denticles—small, tooth-like scales that cover some types of fish

dorsal fin—a fin on the back of a fish

electric field—a wave of electricity created by movement; every living being has an electric field.

lateral lines—a system of tubes beneath a shark's skin that helps it detect changes in water pressure

mature—to become able to reproduce

migrate—to move from one place to another, often with the seasons

ovoviviparous—producing young that develop in eggs inside the body; ovoviviparous animals give birth to live young.

pectoral fins—a pair of fins that extend from each side of a fish's body

serrated—having a jagged edge

temperate—neither too warm nor too cold

torpedo—a rocket-shaped weapon designed to glide easily through the water; torpedoes are used to sink ships and submarines.

uterus—a protective chamber inside some female animals; great white sharks develop in eggs inside the mother's uterus.

vulnerable—at risk of becoming endangered

TO LEARN MORE

At the Library

Musgrave, Ruth. *National Geographic Kids Everything Sharks.* Washington, D.C.: National Geographic, 2011.

Owings, Lisa. *The Great White Shark.* Minneapolis, Minn.: Bellwether Media, Inc., 2012.

Randolph, Joanne. *The Great White Shark: King of the Ocean.* New York, N.Y.: PowerKids Press, 2007.

On the Web

Learning more about great white sharks is as easy as 1, 2, 3.

1. Go to www.factsurfer.com.

2. Enter "great white sharks" into the search box.

3. Click the "Surf" button and you will see a list of related Web sites.

With factsurfer.com, finding more information is just a click away.

INDEX

Women's Health

TOTAL
FITNESS
GUIDE
2009

Women'sHealth
TOTAL
FITNESS
GUIDE
2009
YOUR FITTEST YEAR STARTS NOW!

From the Editors of Women'sHealth Magazine

RODALE

Book design by Joanna Williams

ISBN 13: 978–1–60529–009–6

ISBN 10: 1–60529–009–2

2   4   6   8   10   9   7   5   3   1   hardcover

We inspire and enable people to improve their lives and the world around them

For more of our products visit **rodalestore.com** or call 800-848-4735

contents

contents

contents

■ **PART ONE**

getting started

Before starting any fitness plan, you need to know where you stand in terms of overall fitness and what goals you want to achieve. The tests, goal-setting strategies, and workouts that follow will get you on the road to the body you want in no time!

CHAPTER ONE

CRUNCH YOUR NUMBERS

HOW FIT ARE YOU? TAKE THESE HIGH-TECH TESTS, THEN ACE YOUR FITNESS GOALS.

BY LARA ROSENBAUM

THE LAST TIME YOU found yourself in a lab, you were probably fumbling with a Bunsen burner and flirting with your chem partner. Well, a new trend in fitness is about to land you back there—as a specimen.

Lablike fitness testing centers are popping up at U.S. gyms to give you high-tech insights into how in shape you really are. To get the lowdown, we sussed out the four most widely available tests and asked Jack Daniels, Ph.D. (cocktails, anyone?), head distance coach at the Center for High Altitude Training at Northern Arizona University, how best to use them. "It's most important to retest every few months—using the same variables, such as location, equipment, and time—and tweak your workout accordingly," Daniels says. Here are all the deets you need, from what the tests measure to how to take them—and why tracking the results is key to nailing your fitness goals.

VO$_2$ Max Test

WHO SHOULD TAKE IT Anyone training for an endurance event, like a marathon, a century ride, or a triathlon

WHAT IT TELLS YOU The amount of oxygen your body converts into energy during each minute of maxed-out exercise. The higher the number, the more aerobically fit you are.

WHAT YOU'LL SUFFER THROUGH A nearly puke-inducing all-out effort. You get on a treadmill or a stationary bike wearing a heart-rate monitor and a funky mask hooked up to a computer to track your breathing and oxygen intake. You start out easy, but after the first minute, the administrator juices the speed every 60 seconds until you're not sure you can continue; then you maintain that intensity for another dreadful minute. A computer spits out your score. Genetics and conditions like asthma can affect your number, so the point is to get a baseline.

HOW TO USE THE RESULTS The average O$_2$ intake for healthy women ages 26 to 35 is between 35 and 50 milliliters per kilogram per minute; an elite female athlete's could be in the 60s or above. You can raise your number by up to 20 percent if you increase your cardio 3 percent every three to four weeks.

WHERE TO FIND IT High-end gyms around the country. You can also check out vo2maxtesting .net for an online directory of locations.

Expect to shell out $120 to $125.

Resting Metabolic Rate (RMR) Test

WHO SHOULD TAKE IT Anyone

WHAT IT TELLS YOU The number of calories your body burns at rest

WHAT YOU'LL SUFFER THROUGH You need to be as inactive as possible—which means no heart-rate-raising activities and no food for at least 3 hours before the test. Once in the lab, you recline in a chair and breathe into a long tube for 10 minutes while a computer records how much oxygen you inhale and how much carbon dioxide you exhale.

HOW TO USE THE RESULTS This program tells you how many calories you can eat each day without adding or losing weight. To shed a jeans size, cut your daily caloric intake by up to 15 percent. Athletes should add calories to their baseline to build or maintain muscle.

WHERE TO FIND IT Call around to local gyms or sports nutritionists (find one at eatright.org) to find one providing RMR testing.

Expect to shell out $55 to $100.

Wingate Anaerobic Test

WHO SHOULD TAKE IT Anyone who breaks a sweat in sports that require short bursts of energy, like soccer, tennis, or volleyball

WHAT IT TELLS YOU How long and hard you can sprint—aka anaerobic power. The slower you fatigue, the better conditioned you are.

WHAT YOU'LL SUFFER THROUGH You start out with a warmup: pedaling a no-frills stationary bike for 5 minutes. After a 5-minute rest, you hop back in the saddle and pedal as fast as you can. The administrator eyeballs your speed; when it stops increasing, she cranks the resistance until it's tough for you to maintain that speed. Next, she starts the clock and you pedal as hard and as fast as you can for 30 more grueling seconds. A computer analyzes your pedal strokes and churns out your power-generation results.

HOW TO USE THE RESULTS To up your score, talk to a trainer about adding plyometrics—moves that train you for explosive power—to your workout. Retest every 3 to 6 months.

WHERE TO FIND IT Health clubs that offer sport-specific training. Find the one nearest you at gympost.com or check out your local university. Many sports science departments offer the test to the public for a fee.

Expect to shell out $35 to $99.

Body Fat Percentage Test

WHO SHOULD TAKE IT Anyone

WHAT IT TELLS YOU The proportion of your body mass that's made of fat. Basically, it's D-Day if you're a Mickey D's regular.

WHAT YOU'LL SUFFER THROUGH A trainer or technician uses a skin-fold caliper—that tong-like gizmo—to pinch your triceps, your tummy just above your hip, and the front of your thigh, among other areas. "There are lots of expensive ways to determine body composition," Daniels says. "But results from traditional skin-fold calipers are just as accurate, and they're the cheapest method."

HOW TO USE THE RESULTS A fit woman should have 14 to 25 percent body fat. Anything more, and you should rethink your diet and workout. Under 14 percent? Eat! Too little body fat can lead to funky periods and low bone density.

WHERE TO FIND IT Your local gym. Many facilities offer the service free with membership. Or, to keep tabs on your own body fat, splurge for the Tanita Ironman BC-558 Body Composition Monitor ($300, tanita.com for stores). It tells you the percentage of muscle, water, and fat in your core and extremities.

Expect to shell out $5 to $15 (if you're not a gym member or if your gym charges a fee).

MAXED OUT

See how your VO$_2$ max measures up against the world's best athletes

35–50*
Average woman

83.8
Lance Armstrong, seven-time Tour de France winner

94
Björn Daehlie, Norwegian cross-country skier

240
Alaskan huskies running in the Iditarod Trail Sled Dog Race

* All units measured in ml/kg/min

PART ONE: GETTING STARTED

CHAPTER TWO

WORKOUT
CHRONICLES

TO NAIL YOUR FITNESS GOALS FASTER, TRY LIFTING A PEN.

BY PAIGE GREENFIELD

WORKING OUT is really a competition—against yourself. And the best way to know if you're winning is to track your progress. Sounds great, except it's hard enough to remember to pack a sports bra, much less recall how much weight you hoisted last Tuesday. That's why you've gotta write it down. Every detail you put on paper will let you know when to scale back and when to jack it up a notch. Even better, you'll know you're getting fitter. We talked to fitness gurus to find out the five most important things you should record after every workout. Any pad will do (our pick: the very cute Hable Construction spiral-top notebook, $16, seejanework.com). Tackle all your goals just by jotting down a few notes? We'll ink that deal.

Log this:
Date, Day, Time, Location, and Whatever Strength Moves or Cardio You Do That Day

TO FIGURE OUT: Your ideal workout conditions

HOW TO USE THE INTEL: At the end of every week, place a star by the days you were especially productive and an "X" by the ones when you felt like hell. After a month, note the trends and adjust your schedule accordingly. "Maybe you'll notice that you can lift more weight first thing in the morning and push yourself harder on the track after work," says Kelli Calabrese, M.S., C.S.C.S., a trainer in Flower Mound, Texas. (Yes, that's the name of her town. We asked—twice.)

Log this:
Reps, Sets, and Weights

TO FIGURE OUT: How to tweak your strength workout to achieve max results

HOW TO USE THE INTEL: To keep improving strength and tone, you need to up the number of sets, reps, or the weight each time you do a particular workout. Whichever you choose, increase that same factor across the board, like this: If last week you did one set each of 8, 10, and 12 reps per exercise, today aim for 10, 12, and 15 reps. This might sound like a big fat duh, but when you're doing 10 different exercises in a workout, it's hard to remember info like this, says Pamela Peeke, M.D., M.P.H., author of *Fit to Live*. "It takes the thinking out of it and helps you set goals, so every workout you're challenging yourself a little more," Calabrese says.

Log this:
Intensity

TO FIGURE OUT: Whether you're doing your best

HOW TO USE THE INTEL: After each set of a strength exercise, note your Perceived Exertion (PE)—how hard you worked on a scale from 1 to 10 (1 feels like you could do a hundred more reps, and at 10 you're shaking to eke out the last rep). After a cardio workout, write down your max PE (1 = You can chat easily; 10 = Speak? Ha!) and how much time you spent at that level. Too subjective for you? Record the percentage of your maximum heart rate (MHR = 220 minus your age) you reached for a sustained period during the work-

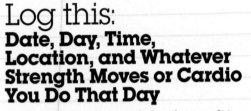

out. If your efforts don't rise above 7 on the PE scale or 60 to 85 percent of your MHR, it's time to challenge yourself more.

Log this:
Energy Index

TO FIGURE OUT: Whether you're about to break up with your fitness plan

HOW TO USE THE INTEL: Women whose primary workout motivation is weight loss spend 40 percent less time exercising than those who do it for other reasons, like maintaining overall health and relieving stress, according to a 2006 University of Michigan study. To make sure your regimen is making you happy, note your Energy Index (EI): how you feel on a scale of 1 to 5, with 1 being in the dumps and 5 being ready for anything. Also note the reason for the number you selected: Were you sore? Tired? Agitated? Eyeball the chart every Sunday. If your score dips below a 3 for five workouts in a row, one of a few things is happening: You're overdoing it, you're slacking, or you're stinking bored. The bottom line: It's time to tweak your routine. Instead of the treadmill, try a step or kickboxing class, or do a circuit: Between sets, jump rope, run in place, do jumping jacks or knee lifts—for 1 minute.

Log this:
Body Fat

To find out: How much fat you're replacing with muscle

HOW TO USE THE INTEL: Watching your body fat shrink is proof that you're getting not only stronger but also healthier, since excess body fat increases your risk of heart disease, stroke, and type 2 diabe-

NOW ONLINE
TRACK YOUR WORKOUTS WITH *WH!*

Starting January 1, you'll be able to sign up for our 2nd annual Women's Health Ultimate Fitness Plan at womenshealthmag.com/fitplan. Just like last year's Fitness Plan, this one is an expert-developed, totally doable 6-month program for getting in the best shape of your life. What's new for '09, however, is that you'll get a password to access your own online fitness journal. This means you'll be able to enter and save information about each workout you do—including the "Log This" items mentioned here—so you can carefully track your progress. And, even better, it's free!

tes. Use this number to motivate yourself to get your ever-more-chiseled butt to the workout room. Many gyms have "bioelectrical impedance analysis" scales that compute your body fat percentage by tracking how quickly an electrical current travels through your body (don't worry, you won't feel a thing). Because muscles are nearly 70 percent water and fat contains almost no H_2O, the faster the signal travels, the more muscle you have. Don't have access to one of these scales? Use a measuring tape to calculate the circumference of your waist at the belly button. Say it comes out to 30 inches, and last month it was 32. That's 2 inches of fat you've lost—fat that's being replaced by muscle, which takes up less room. Either way, measure and log this number only once a month: That's about how long it can take to achieve a noticeable change.

DECODE YOUR DISPLAY

FOR A SMARTER, MORE EFFECTIVE WORKOUT, FOLLOW THIS ANNOTATED GUIDE TO YOUR MACHINE'S DASHBOARD.

BY JENNY EVERETT

BETWEEN ABSORBING THE GOSSIP on tmz.com and the dramas of a certain overchatty co-worker (Her boyfriend has a bunion! Her tampon feels funny!), your brain has become bloated with useless knowledge. Oh, and then there's your cardio machine, blinking at you with unbridled enthusiasm. Welcome to the too-much-information age. But when it comes to fitness, paying attention to the minutiae is key to getting in shape and staying there. So we polled trainers and M.D.s to find out which details on the average machine's data-plastered dashboard you need to know to get a great workout—and the body that comes with it.

3. Check Your Progress

Note your average speed (most bikes flash this stat on the large display area post-workout), suggests Tom Holland, M.S., C.S.C.S., owner of TeamHolland in Darien, Connecticut. Try to increase that average each pedal-fest. The most effective game plan: intervals. Alternate sprints at, say, 20 to 25 mph with recoveries at 15 mph.

4. Pedal Faster

Keep your revolutions per minute (rpm) over 60. When you just slog along, you don't get into a good rhythm, and that can make you more liable to lose your form. Try this routine: Pick a range, like 70 to 80 rpm, and try to stay within it for 5 minutes. Next, blast over 100 for 1 minute. Then recover at 60 to 80 rpm for 1 minute. Repeat three to five times.

Your Machine: The Bike

1. Tweak Your MPH

To mimic your outdoor routine, pick a speed 5 to 10 miles per hour faster than your average speed on the road. With no wind or varied terrain to contend with, doing anything less is slacking.

2. Don't Be a Dork

No need to pay attention to watts or METS. These are measures of power (literally, how much electricity you'd produce if you were hooked up to a genera-tor) and energy that are only useful to elite athletes.

AFG 4.0 AH

COOL FEATURE
Hybrid upright/recumbent design goes easy on the joints without messing with your rep.

PRICE
$1,499

GET IT
advancedfitnessgroup.com for stores

Your Machine: The Elliptical

1. Test Yourself

To gauge your progress, take this test every 4 weeks: See how many strides you can complete in 10 minutes within your target heart-rate zone. Or, if the machine has a built-in fitness test—as many brand-new models do—try that instead.

2. Let Your Rate Rule

Elliptical machines feel so smooth and comfy, it's easy to doubt that you're actually getting a workout. Ignore the calories (which are okay as a benchmark but aren't entirely accurate, as they don't take room conditions into account) and focus on stride rate (number of times per minute your legs go around). If you're not averaging at least 160, you're not racking up cardio benefits.

3. Cross-train Smarter

Adjust the angle of incline based on the sport you're training for, suggests Emily Cooper, M.D., founder of Seattle Performance Medicine in Seattle. For hiking, set it at 7 to 10 percent to mimic trail conditions and make your glutes do the brunt of the work. For cycling, set it at 4 to 6 percent to work your hamstrings and quads, the pedaling muscles. For running, set it at 1 to 4 percent to target your quads and calves.

4. Take It in Stride

The elliptical's sweetest feature is that you can adjust your stride—usually in half-inch incre-ments from 18 to 26 inches. Generally, someone under 5'5" should stay below 22 inches; taller people can go up to 26 inches.

OCTANE Q47

COOL FEATURE
Adjustable stride length

PRICE
$3,599

GET IT
octanefitness.com for stores

Your Machine: The Treadmill

1. Pooh-Pooh the Fat-Burning Program

This setting is based on heart-rate ranges for less fit users—so for the average woman who works out a few times a week, it will be far too easy. To truly fry fat, set it to "manual" and do this: Sprint for 2 minutes, then recover for 30 to 60 seconds. Repeat six times. During the sprint sessions, aim for at least 85 percent of your maximum heart rate (220 minus your age times 0.85).

2. Angle for Results

Your incline should always be set to at least 1 percent. Always, even during cooldown. Because there's less resistance on a treadmill than there is running on, say, the road, the incline will more accurately simulate actual running, according to *Women's Health* columnist Amy Dixon, exercise physiologist and group fitness manager for Equinox in Santa Monica, California.

3. Go with the Beat

Get your heart rate up to 10 to 15 beats per minute higher than it is when you run outside. Why? Your indoor heart rate is jacked, thanks to higher humidity and zero wind inside. The extra BPMs will keep you at your normal exertion level.

4. Give Good Info

Most machines are calibrated to a 180-pound adult. If you tip the scale either way, you have to enter your weight for an accurate calories-burned reading, says Heather Guymon, exercise physiologist and certified personal trainer in Logan, Utah.

LIFEFITNESS PLATINUM CLUB SERIES TREADMILL

COOL FEATURES
A virtual trainer and an iPod hookup

PRICE
$7,999

GET IT
lifefitness.com for stores

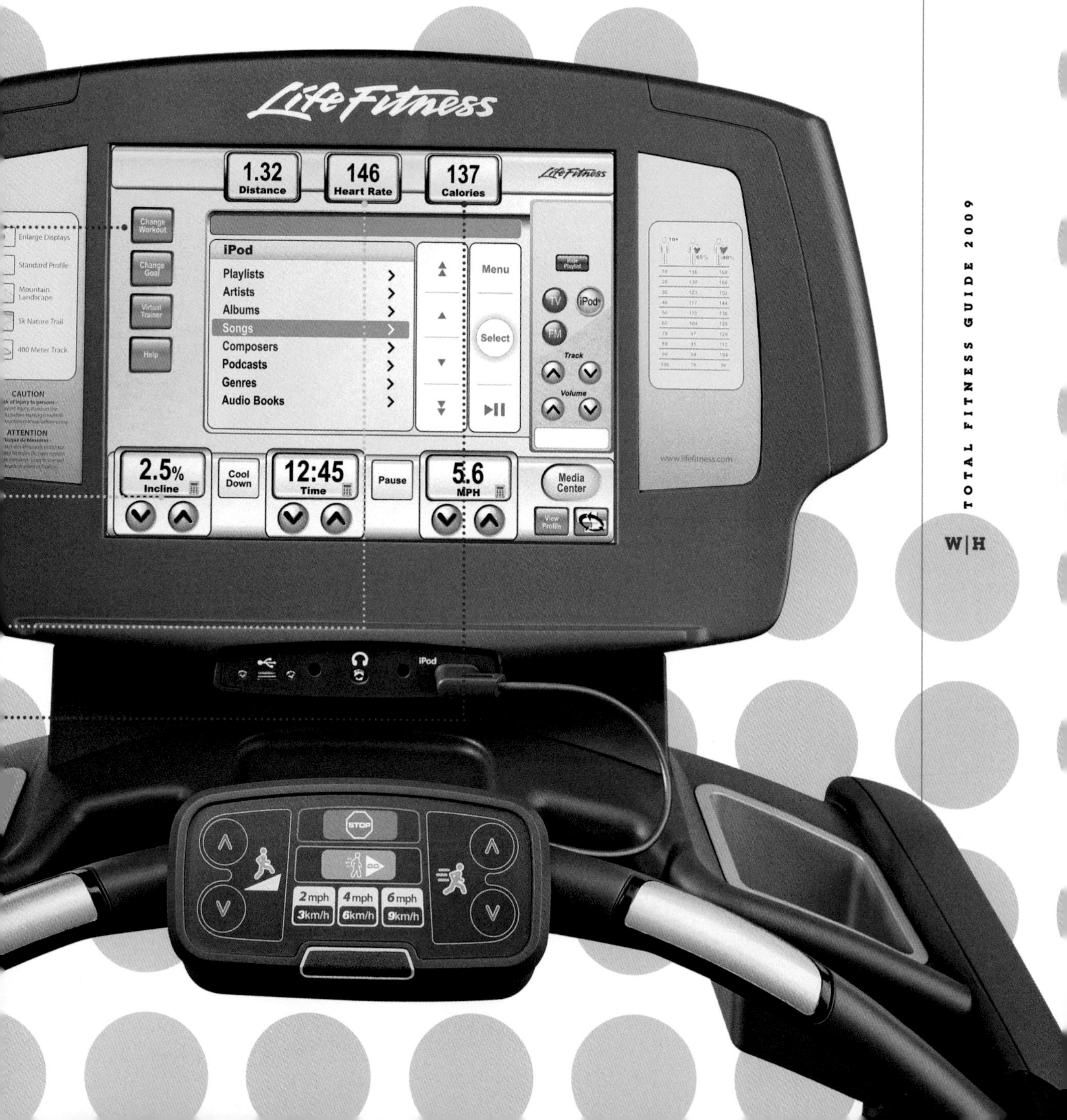

W | H

Life Fitness

| 1.32 | 146 | 137 |
| Distance | Heart Rate | Calories |

Enlarge Displays

Standard Profile

Mountain Landscape

5k Nature Trail

400 Meter Track

CAUTION

ATTENTION

Change Workout

Change Goal

Virtual Trainer

Help

iPod

Playlists
Artists
Albums
Songs
Composers
Podcasts
Genres
Audio Books

Menu

Select

►II

Hide Playlist

TV   iPod

FM

Track

Volume

www.lifefitness.com

| 2.5% | Cool Down | 12:45 | Pause | 5.6 | Media Center |
| Incline | | Time | | MPH | |

View Profile

USB   headphone   iPod

STOP

GO

| 2 mph | 4 mph | 6 mph |
| 3km/h | 6km/h | 9km/h |

CHAPTER FOUR

31 DAYS OF FITNESS

STAYING FIT DURING DECEMBER ISN'T IMPOSSIBLE. REALLY. JUST STICK TO OUR EXPERT-APPROVED, TOTALLY DOABLE DAY-TO-DAY PLAN, AND YOU'LL BREAK INTO '09 AS FIT AND STRONG AS EVER–MAYBE EVEN STRONGER.

BY DIMITY McDOWELL

REPEAT AFTER US: "The Grinch will not steal my fitness this year."

In fact, we guarantee that if you plot your December according to our calendar, you can maintain your mojo—and even improve it. And that doesn't mean adding an unrealistic number of workouts to your holiday schedule. Earlier this year, the American College of Sports Medicine fine-tuned its 30-minutes-a-day, most-days-a-week Rx to one that suggests 20 minutes of vigorous aerobic exercise 3 days a week, plus two 1-set strength sessions.

Since 'tis the season of endless cookie platters, we created a plan that emphasizes calorie crushing and weight training. What follows is a calendar with not only expert-designed strength and cardio workouts but also smart, simple tips for squeezing in more exercise and deep-sixing stress. Consider it our gift certificate for a fitter, stronger you. It expires on December 31, so redeem immediately. We'll look for your thank-you notes in the mail.

KEY *Moves on pages 24–31*

STRENGTH

TREADMILL

BIKE

Week One

1. Call on Karma

Just because Race for the Cure is on a holiday hiatus doesn't mean you can't sweat for a good cause. Today, find out when the Jingle Bell Run/Walk, a 5K held in 110 cities nationwide to benefit the Arthritis Foundation, comes to your 'hood. Then get ready to don your Donner costume and dash through it. ($20 to $30 entry fee, arthritis.org)

2. Warm Up Your Credit Card

Nothing says "Get off your ass!" better than the prospect of slipping into a slick new gym outfit, says Amie Hoff, a fitness consultant at New York Sports Clubs. But no wearing it yet; you have to earn it (see Friday the 25th). Wrap it up and stick it under the tree. Our suggestion: Lululemon's crop slit boogie pants, which turn all shapes of rears into booty-licious glutes, and the stylish Whisper tank. ($69 for pants, $48 for tank; lululemon.com)

3. Had Enough of Bing Already?

Before tackling your first workout, go to womenshealthmag.com/playlists and download these holiday songs that don't suck.

"Christmas Wrapping" The Waitresses

"Merry Christmas (I Don't Want to Fight Tonight)" The Ramones

"Father Christmas" The Kinks

"Step into Christmas" Elton John

"The Christmas Song" (Holiday Remix) Christina Aguilera

"Christmas (Baby Please Come Home)" U2

"Elf's Lament" Barenaked Ladies

"I've Got My Love to Keep Me Warm" (Stuhr Remix) Kay Starr

"Last Christmas" (Studio Remix) Jimmy Eat World

"This Year Will Be My Year" Semisonic

4. The 1st Day of Strength Training

(See page 24 for workout plan.) Do the routine straight through, twice, without rest.

5. Step It Up

You could wait for the elevator, enduring holiday Muzak, or you could opt for the stairs. Go with the latter: Not only do you burn 10 calories a minute hoofing it up and down (compared with, um, 1 calorie for standing), it takes less than half the time to get from one floor to the next, according to a 2007 University of South Carolina study.

6. The 2nd Day of Strength Training

Do 1 set. In between exercises, jump rope for 1 minute. Don't have one? Try Buddy Lee's Master Rope. You can adjust the length to suit your size, and bearings in the handles create a smooth, dragless motion. ($28, buddyleejumpropes.com)

7. Treadmill Workout

Week Two

8. The 3rd Day of Strength Training

Do 2 sets, resting 30 to 60 seconds in between. In the step and plank move, add a pushup when you're in plank position.

9. Give Some Retail Therapy

Schlepping shopping bags, shoveling snow, double-clicking your way to the primo present: The holidays are kink-inducing times. The Trigger Point Starter Set includes a spongy ball with a dense core and a dumbbell-size roller to mimic a real massage—making it the perfect gift for carpal tunnel sufferers, stressed-out bosses, and (literal) pains in the neck. Gift the roller, but keep the ball for yourself. ($70, tptherapy.com)

10. The 4th Day of Strength Training

Do 1 set. Between exercises, run up and down a flight of stairs, or step up and down on a step for 1 minute.

11. Log Your Miles

Shop. Your entire day of searching for some creepily lifelike doll for your niece is a workout. Want proof? Pick up Polar's AW200 Activity Watch, a fab (if pricey) gadget that measures all forward motion in steps, as well as altitude climbed and descended and calories burned. Its internal accelerometer can pick up even the lightest movement and detect its intensity—making pedometers look seriously JV ($200, polarusa.com. Or, if you kicked your cash on said robot doll, go to womenshealthmag.com for a chance to win one.)

12. The 5th Day of Strength Training

Do 2 sets, resting 30 to 60 seconds in between. In each move that has a one-legged element, stay balanced for 2 counts before moving on to the next exercise.

13. Bike Workout

14. The 6th Day of Strength Training

Do only 1 set. Then take a Pilates class to stretch everything out. Go to healthclubdirectory.com to find one in your area.

Week Three

15. Stoke Your Slope Skills

Order your own copy of the new DVD Labor of Love, the first-ever action-sports film featuring women—there's not a single dude—utterly shredding the slopes. The flick stars 2007 X Games gold medalists Sarah Burke and Torah Bright. If these two badasses don't motivate you to bomb down the mountain, nothing will. ($20, roxy.com)

16. Start Wrapping: Christmas Is Just 9 Days Away!

When you do, give your body a present too. "You're usually hunched over when you wrap, which wreaks havoc on your back," says Linda Taix, owner of Extreme Boot Camp in La Canada, California. So after you tie each bow perfectly, de-hunch by doing 30 crunches and 20 donkey kicks (rest on your elbows and knees, kick heel to glutes) on each side.

17. Treadmill Workout

18. The 7th Day of Strength Training

Do 2 sets, resting 30 to 60 seconds in between. Ditch the weights and concentrate on perfect form.

19. End the Day Upside-Down

To calm your mind and relax your body, get into shoulder stand (visit iyogalife.com for video instruction). When you're inverted, blood rushes to your upper half, your brain included, which promotes relaxation. Once in position, take five deep breaths—count to 4 as you inhale and to 8 as you exhale—then bend your knees toward your forehead and slowly roll down. "After that, you'll be so mellow you won't care if your boyfriend buys you a blender," says Lawson Harris, owner of Half Moon Pilates in New York City.

20. The 8th Day of Strength Training

Do 20 minutes of cardio first. Push the intensity to the point where you can talk but it's easier just to concentrate on breathing. Then do 1 set of strength training.

21. Redline Your Muscles with Rudolph's Schnoz

Tune in to *Rudolph the Red-Nosed Reindeer*, and every time his nose lights up, drop to the floor and

do 10 pushups. "Position your hands directly below your shoulders," says Tanja Djelevic, owner of Loud Fitness in Los Angeles. "As you lower toward the ground, your elbows should go backward, not out to the side." At the top, tuck your tailbone—tilt your pelvis slightly forward—for a mini-crunch. Avoid beelining for the cutout cookies by jumping rope during commercials.

Week Four

22. The 9th Day of Strength Training

Do 2 sets, resting 30 to 60 seconds in between. Instead of 10 to 12 reps for each exercise, make it 15.

23. Climb Mother Nature's Stairmaster

Then sled down the hill you just ascended. Continue doing laps on the hill for an hour, and you'll burn nearly 340 calories (about four candy canes' worth). Our sled of choice: the Airboard Softboard, a plastic inflatable sled that's way speedier (and cooler) than the dented-up, dusty silver saucer in your garage. ($129, airboard.com)

24. The 10th Day of Strength Training 🏋️

Do 2 sets, resting 30 to 60 seconds in between. Perform each exercise for 1 minute. Recover for 15 seconds before moving to the next one.

25. Really, I Shouldn't Have . . .

Open the outfit you stashed under the tree on the 2nd—surprise!—as you commit to completing the month of fitness. Just. Six. More. Days. To. Go.

26. The 11th Day of Strength Training 🏋️

Do 2 sets, resting 30 to 60 seconds in between. Keep your muscles progressing by reversing the exercise order.

27. Bike Workout 🚲

28. The 12th Day of Strength Training 🏋️

Do 3 sets, resting 30 to 60 seconds in between. It's the last workout of the month: Finish strong.

Week Five
(A Short One!)

29. Sip a Steaming Cup of Recovery

Head out for a snowshoe or cross-country ski, then refuel with a Clif Shot hot chocolate-flavored protein-spiked drink. It tastes just like the real thing but has 6 grams of protein and 23 grams of carbs per 140-calorie packet—perfect to get you reloaded for the afternoon's snowball fight. ($1.70 for an 8-ounce packet, clifbar.com)

30. Forget the "Lose 10 Pounds" BS

And resolve to do something specific: a 10K, a metric century (62 miles on a bike), or a sprint-distance triathlon (find an event at active.com). "Before you dive into structured training, though, make sure you've established a base of regular activity so you don't end up injured, sore, and unmotivated—or some combination thereof," says Dorette Sommer, a USA Triathlon-certified coach and owner of East Peak Sports in San Francisco, who offers these guidelines:

10K

PREREQ Run three to four times a week, building up to 45 minutes per run, for 6 weeks. (If you want to run three times, cross-train once weekly.)

Then really train for 8 to 10 weeks.

METRIC CENTURY

PREREQ Ride three times a week—two shorter rides of 45 to 60 minutes, one longer one that gradually builds to 3 hours—for 6 weeks.

Then really train for 12 weeks.

SPRINT TRIATHLON (0.5 MILE SWIM, 12.4-MILE BIKE, 3.1-MILE RUN)

PREREQ Each week for 6 to 8 weeks, do three 30-minute swims, two 45-minute rides, and three 30-minute runs. On weekends, do two workouts: swim then bike, or bike then run.

Then really train for 12 weeks.

31. Suck Face

We were going to tell you to do crunches for the entire countdown to '09. But we resolved to stop being so bitchy. So instead, ignore mood-killer Dick Clark, and make out with your man—you'll burn slightly more than one calorie per minute. Make it an all-nighter and, well, you do the math.

Tone for the Holidays

These moves from Patrick Goudeau, a certified personal trainer in Los Angeles who stars in the *DVD Hard Work Conditioning*, will give you a complete strength workout—and get your heart muscle pumping, too. In short: Calories will be toast. Follow the instructions for each calendar day, but always use 5- to 12-pound dumbbells and aim for 10 to 12 reps per set.

LUNGE LIFT

WORKS BICEPS, GLUTES, INNER THIGHS, AND QUADS

Grab a pair of dumbbells and stand with them at your sides. Take a giant step back with your left foot and lower your hips until your right thigh is parallel to the floor (A). Raise the dumbbells toward your body until your thumbs are within an inch of your shoulders (B). Lower the weights and straighten your right leg while bringing your left knee forward—keeping it bent—until your thigh is level with your hip. Raise the dumbbells again (C). Lower the weights and your leg. Complete all reps, then switch sides.

A   B   C

SIDE SWEEP

WORKS SHOULDERS AND INNER
AND OUTER THIGHS

Grab a dumbbell in your right hand and position your
feet wider than shoulder-width apart. Bend your left
knee 90 degrees and keep your right leg straight.
Bending forward at the waist with a straight spine,
touch the dumbbell to the floor, next to the inside of
your left foot, and extend your left arm straight behind
you at shoulder height (A). Push off your left foot and
stand up so you're balancing on your right foot with
your left leg bent 90 degrees, thigh at hip level. At the
same time, extend your right arm out to the side at
shoulder height and your left arm straight up to the
ceiling (B). Complete all reps, then switch sides.

A

B

TOTAL FITNESS GUIDE 2009

W | H

TURKISH GET-UP

WORKS CORE

Grab a dumbbell with your right hand. Lie on your
back with your right leg flat on the floor and your left
leg bent with your foot flat on the floor. Raise your
right leg about 2 inches and extend your right arm
straight up so it's perpendicular to your body, palm in.
Extend your left arm straight out to the side (A). Brace
your abs and curl up to sitting without lowering your
right leg (B). Slowly lower yourself back down.
Complete all reps, then switch sides.

A

B

UP AND OVER

WORKS SHOULDERS, LATS, AND OBLIQUES

Grab a dumbbell with your right hand and stand with your feet slightly wider than hip width, your left arm a few inches from your side. Hold the dumbbell an inch in front of your right shoulder (A). Extend your right arm overhead as you bend your torso to the left. Keep going until you feel as if you're about to tip over (B). As you straighten back up, sweep your left arm to the side and overhead. Lower the dumbbell so it's back in front of your shoulder (C). Complete all reps, then switch sides.

A   B   C

W|H

EXTEND-O-CRUNCH

WORKS SHOULDERS, BICEPS, AND ABS

Grab a dumbbell in each hand and lie on your back.
Bend your knees 90 degrees and lift your legs until
your calves are perpendicular to the floor. With palms
facing each other, position the weights a few inches
above your chest. Crunch up slightly, so your
shoulders are off the ground (A). Straighten and
lower your right leg so it's hovering above the floor; at
the same time, reach both hands overhead so your
arms are in line with your ears (B). Pull everything
back in and repeat. Complete all reps, then switch
sides.

A

B

DOUBLE EXTENSION

WORKS SHOULDERS, TRICEPS, LOWER BACK, AND GLUTES

Grab a dumbbell in your right hand and get on all fours. Lift your elbow toward the ceiling until your arm is bent 90 degrees (A). Contract your triceps and straighten your right arm behind you so it's in line with your torso (B). Bend it back to 90 degrees, then extend it forward in line with your shoulder while extending your left leg behind you (C). Complete all reps, then switch sides.

A

B

C

STEP AND PLANK

WORKS CHEST, ABS, GLUTES, AND
INNER THIGHS

Grab a dumbbell in each hand and stand with your
arms at your sides. Take a big step back with your
right leg so that your left leg is bent 90 degrees. Lean
forward from the hips and lower the weights until
they're on the floor on either side of your left foot (A).
Step back with your left leg into plank position (B).
Hold for 2 seconds. Bring your left foot up between
your hands and squeeze your glutes to stand back up.
Complete all reps, then switch sides.

A

B

Dash Through the Snow

Annette Hudson, a certified personal trainer and the owner of My Fitness Trainer in Puyallup, Washington, designed this treadmill workout for runners and walkers. It uses varying degrees of incline to target lower leg muscles. Slowly increase your speed to a moderate level and try to maintain that speed throughout the workout.

MINUTES	0-5	5-7	7-8	8-10	10-13	13-15	15-19	19-33	33-38
EFFORT*	5	7	6	8	6	7	6	Repeat minutes 5-19	4
INCLINE	1%	4%	1%	6%	1%	4%	1%		1%

Spin Zone

Like the treadmill workout, this cycling routine, from Tom Holland, M.S., C.S.C.S., tweaks resistance and intensity throughout, so your muscles never get a break. Quick and effective—just our style.

MINUTES	0-5	5-8	8-9	9-10	10-14	14-18
EFFORT*	5	6	8	5	Do 8-10 twice	6
CADENCE** (revolutions per minute)	80-90	80-90	60-80	90-100		80-90
RESISTANCE	Low	Medium	High (Stand and climb)	Low		Medium

MINUTES	18-21X	21-23	23-23:30	23:30-24	24-26	26-30 Cool Down
EFFORT*	9	5	10	3 (Stand and pedal)	Do 23-24 twice	5
CADENCE** (revolutions per minute)	80-90	60-80	90-100	60-80		80-90
RESISTANCE	Medium-high	Low	Medium	High		Very low

* On a scale of 1 to 10: 1 is "I could do this all day"; at 5 you can still speak in full sentences; 8 allows you to speak in spurts of 3 or 4 words; and 10 pretty much sucks.
** To calculate rpm, count the number of times your right leg goes around in 15 seconds and multiply that number by 4.

CHAPTER FIVE

WORK OUT THE KINKS

PREVENT MUSCLE MUTINY WITH THESE FOUR FEEL-GOOD MOVES.

MOST OF THE TIME, a good workout makes you feel superbadass. But sometimes you wind up feeling superbad. Key culprits: your back, knees, neck, and shoulders—which can suffer from muscle imbalances (when one muscle gets stronger while its opposing muscle gets weaker). This sets you up for injury. For an ouch-free session, start your workout with these four joint-stabilizing moves from Scott Lucett, director of education at the National Academy of Sports Medicine.

The Moves

BALL SQUAT WITH TUBING

PAIN-PRONE AREA: FRONTS AND SIDES OF THE KNEES

Stand with your feet shoulder-width apart and wrap resistance tubing around your knees so there's no slack in the band. Place a stability ball between the middle of your back and a wall, but put only enough pressure on it to keep the ball from falling. Squat down as if sitting on a chair, pushing out against the tubing to keep your knees from caving inward. Press back up to start. Do two sets of 12 reps, resting for 30 to 60 seconds between sets.

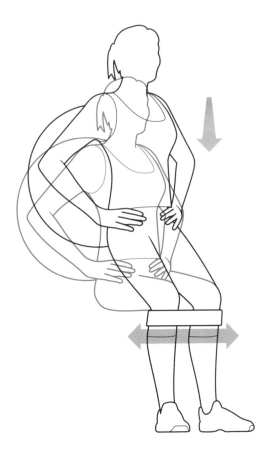

BALL BRIDGE

PAIN-PRONE AREA: LOWER BACK

Rest your upper back on a stability ball with your feet hip-width apart on the floor. Your shoulders, hips, and knees should be aligned horizontally, like a table. Brace your abs and lower your hips until your butt hovers 3 to 6 inches above the floor. Squeeze your glutes and lift your hips back to the starting position. Do two sets of 12 reps, resting for 30 to 60 seconds between sets.

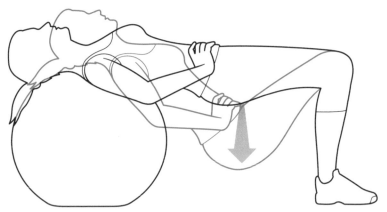

SWAN NECK

PAIN-PRONE AREA: SIDES OF THE NECK

Keeping your head level, slowly draw it straight back, keeping your chin parallel to the ground (do not drop your chin toward your chest). Hold for two to three seconds and release. Repeat 10 times. This is the chin position you should maintain during any exercise to ensure proper neck and spine alignment, Lucett says.

BALL COBRA

PAIN-PRONE AREA: FRONTS OF THE SHOULDERS

Lie facedown with your midsection on a stability ball. With your legs hip-width apart, straighten them behind you and press the balls of your feet into the floor. Extend your arms in front of you, palms facing each other, and place your pinkies on the floor. Lift your chest off the ball and pinch your shoulder blades together; at the same time, lift your arms up and out to the sides. Hold for 2 seconds and return to starting position. Do two sets of 12 reps, resting for 30 to 60 seconds between sets.

TOTAL FITNESS GUIDE 2009

W|H

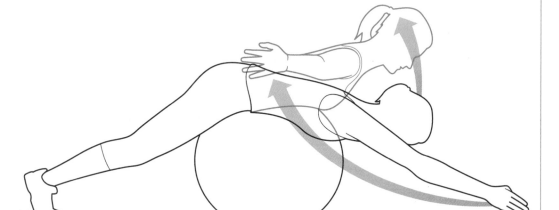

CHAPTER SIX

TUNE IN, TONE UP

GET ON TRACK WITH THESE FOUR PERFORMANCE-GUARANTEED PLAYLISTS.

BY COREY BINNS

MUSIC IS POWERFUL STUFF. You used it in preschool as a learning tool ("A, B, C, D . . . ") and in college as a mood setter ("Your Body Is a Wonderland"). Now it's time to apply it to fitness. In 2005 the North American Association for the Study of Obesity asked a group of women to work up a sweat regularly for 24 weeks, but only half got to listen to tunes during their workouts. The earbud crew lost 16 more pounds and 4 percent more body fat—and were less likely to skip workouts. In other words, they had a serious competitive edge.

But not just any music will do: Tempo, lyrics, and musical style all affect how hard you work. We asked music writer Jim Allen, who has designed hundreds of playlists for MTV and iTunes, to come up with four 40-minute lineups—each one based on the latest lab work—so you get the most out of your moves, whether you're sprinting, spinning, lifting, or asana-ing. Download them and watch your body respond—right on cue.

Yoga/Pilates

PLAYLIST PLAN Relaxing music

WHY IT WORKS In a 2006 study by the Institute of Movement Sciences in Rome, Italy, researchers asked two groups of volunteers to sweat it out on a treadmill for 15 minutes at an intensity comparable to a heart-pumping Power Yoga class. One group listened to upbeat music; the other slogged through the routine in silence. The scientists measured lactic acid, norepinephrine (a stress hormone that shows up in the blood), blood pressure, and heart rate and found that all were significantly lower in the group that worked out with a soundtrack. Their conclusion: Music can chill you out, which makes you better able to concentrate on your form and on transitioning from one move to the next without being distracted by fatigue. To focus on mastering your poses and to practice steady, deep breathing, listen to music with regular, constant rhythms and drumbeats, says Jonathan Fields, cofounder and director of Sonic Yoga in New York City.

QUIET 3 SHEILA
Chandra

SIMPLE THINGS
Zero 7

CHERRY BLOSSOM GIRL
Air

HIDDEN PLACE
Björk

The undulating rhythm is perfect for sun salutations.

THE SEA
Morcheeba

SWEET LULLABY
Deep Forest

SEED AFRO
Celt Sound System

DEVOTIONAL
Tabla Beat Science

Fields plays the drumbeat-driven sounds of this instrumental group in his classes.

NAIMA
Angelique Kidjo
with Carlos Santana

KALULI GROOVE
Mickey Hart
and Zakir Hussain

THANK YOU FOR HEARING ME
Sinéad O'Connor

MUSTT MUSTT (REMIX)
Massive Attack /
Nusrat Fateh Ali Khan

This rhythmic Middle Eastern beat will help you forget any discomfort so you can hold hard poses longer—even when your body is begging for mercy.

Strength Training

PLAYLIST PLAN Strong lyrics

WHY IT WORKS A 2006 study at York St. John University in the U.K. found that students could hold a 2.4-pound weight straight out in front of their bodies at shoulder height for up to 10 percent longer when they listened to motivational pop or rock music for an entire torturous session. The all-music workout beat out listening to white noise and listening to music for only part of the time. But the key is to choose tracks with lyrics that get you amped you up—yes, even if they include the words "Don't Stop Believin'." We think any sane woman would enjoy the motivational ditties at right. But we won't be offended if you decide to sub in a few of your own go-to tunes; pretty much anything you recklessly belt out in the shower or your car is on the money. One tip: Songs that mention specific actions ("Jump!"), particularly those that include body parts ("Put your hands in the air!"), will really light a spark under you when you're struggling to finish that final set of lunges.

LET'S GET LOUD
Jennifer Lopez

YOU'VE GOT ANOTHER THING COMIN'
Judas Priest

JUMP
Van Halen
Great for squats.

Great for squats.

SET ME FREE
Velvet Revolver

JUMP AROUND
House of Pain

KICK OUT THE JAMS
MC5

THE RISING
Bruce Springsteen

BEAUTIFUL DAY (REMIX)
U2

LET'S GO
Trick Daddy

Hearing Bono croon "It's a beautiful day, Don't let it get away" motivated participants in the York St. John University study to hold weights steady up to 10 percent longer.

SOMETHING MORE
Sugarland

RAY OF LIGHT
Madonna

GET UP, STAND UP
Bob Marley

In your final set, take a cue from the reggae master and "Don't give up the fight!"

Spinning

PLAYLIST PLAN Up-tempo tunes

WHY IT WORKS It's not because all spin instructors are ecstasy-loving club kids in disguise. It's because fast music inspires you to move. A 2007 study at Brunel University in London found that runners on a treadmill were more productive when they matched their stride to music with a tempo of 120 to 140 beats per minute (aka bpm—for the average music buff, that's the number of times you tap your foot to a song in one minute). How does this translate to spin class? According to a study by Costas Karageorghis, Ph.D., a senior lecturer in sports psychology at Brunel, you'll work up to 7 percent harder while grooving to music synched to your pedal stroke and not feel any more fatigued. To get the most pedal power from your playlist, Karageorghis recommends songs around 120 bpm for medium to high levels of exertion (when you can speak in spurts of three or four words). When it's time to raise the intensity, bump up your soundtrack to 140.

I'M EVERY WOMAN
Whitney Houston

HIGHER GROUND
Red Hot Chili Peppers

PEOPLE ARE PEOPLE
Depeche Mode

Start at a sane 120 bpm: Studies show you're more productive when a mix starts slow and gets faster later in the workout.

CONTROL
Janet Jackson

HOW BIZARRE
OMC

I WOULDN'T NORMALLY DO THIS KIND OF THING
Pet Shop Boys

Pooped? The next three songs, at 130 to 140 bpm, will help you over the hump.

BLUE MONDAY
New Order

YOU SPIN ME ROUND (LIKE A RECORD)
Dead or Alive

LEGS
ZZ Top

CLOCKS
Coldplay

RUNAROUND
Blues Traveler

MANEATER
Nelly Furtado

Lower your bike's resistance and cool down to this song's slower beat.

Running

PLAYLIST PLAN Power songs

WHY IT WORKS In a 2005 study at Brunel University, 36 runners cut an average of half a second off their 400-meter times when they listened to music in a certain tempo range. Choose tunes in the bpm sweet spot—120 to 140. To kick into high gear when you need it most, pick one fast-paced song (at least 130 bpm) whose lyrics fire you up and position it to play at the point during your run when you usually feel like crap—whether during the warmup or at mile 10. Showing up on Nike's list of 100 power songs requested by women: "Pump It" by the Black Eyed Peas, "The Eye of the Tiger" by Survivor, and Justin Timberlake's "SexyBack." With an iPod Nano ($150, apple.com) and a Nike + Sport Kit ($29, apple.com), you can program your power song to play at the press of a button.

HARDER TO BREATHE •····
Maroon 5

S.O.S.
Rihanna

Use this 136 bpm song to help you set a challenging pace.

ANOTHER ONE BITES THE DUST
Queen

FIRESTARTER •····
The Prodigy

GIRLFRIEND
Avril Lavigne

PUMP IT UP •····
Elvis Costello

THE ROCKAFELLER SKANK
Fatboy Slim

Clocking in at 146 bpm, this song made Nike's list of Top 10 Power Songs on iTunes.

B.O.B. •····
Outkast

SHE WANTS TO MOVE
N.E.R.D.

HERE IT GOES AGAIN •····
OK Go

AROUND THE WORLD
Daft Punk

RUNNIN' DOWN A DREAM •····
Tom Petty

Anything seems possible as you start slowing down with this 115 bpm classic.

TOTAL FITNESS GUIDE 2009

W|H

■ **PART TWO**

total-body strength

Strong, toned bodies come from a combination of training strategies that push your flexibility, balance, muscular strength, endurance, speed, and power. In the pages that follow, you'll find workouts that center on these strategies so you can get that powerful yet toned body.

CHAPTER SEVEN

THIS IS YOUR YEAR!

FIND (AND KEEP) YOUR BEST BODY WITH THE WOMEN'S HEALTH ULTIMATE FITNESS PLAN '09.

BY SELENE YEAGER

LAST YEAR MORE THAN 40,000 women took on our first annual Ultimate Fitness Plan—and they're still bragging about their results. Let their success—and egos—motivate you. This year, no more "Oops, missed a workout," no more "I swear I'll go to the gym—tomorrow," and no more "I'll never have Biel's body." It's our mission to make you look and feel amazing—and this year, it's a done deal.

For the WH Ultimate Fitness Plan '09, we called on the National Academy of Sports Medicine (NASM). The 6-month workout schedule they came up with will transform you—from head to abs to toes. That's because you're going to work out just like the fittest people on the planet do. That's right, you are going to train like an athlete. Why? Because you have the chops, and (if we may appeal to your ego) if you train like an athlete, eventually you'll look like one. And who doesn't want to be lean, strong, and bursting with energy?

Track your results, watch exercise videos (and download them onto your iPod), and get more workouts at womenshealthmag.com/fitplan.

The WH Ultimate Fitness Plan is based on research and guidelines from the fitness gurus at the NASM. The first 8 weeks focus on stabilization exercises that max out your flexibility, core, balance, and alignment to train your brain and muscles to communicate more efficiently. During the second 8 weeks, you'll do exercises that ratchet up your muscular strength, endurance, and, yes, tone. For the last 8 weeks, you'll put the final buff on that body with high-energy athletic moves that build speed and power. Just as with last year's Ultimate Fitness Plan, you'll be breaking a sweat 6 days a week, but every routine fits comfortably into a lunch hour. So no excuses.

Go ahead. Get started. Now!

STEP 1. Figure out how fit you are. On these pages (and at womenshealthmag.com/fitplan) are five fitness challenges designed by the team led by NASM-certified trainer and triathlete Kristi Dowler, owner of VyAyr Fitness led by Women in San Francisco. All you need are a stability ball, a stopwatch, and access to a treadmill (that last one is optional; you can also do the cardio test outside). Take each test, then score yourself accordingly:

Aspiring—Time to tap your potential

Solid—Above average

Strong—Go, athlete!

STEP 2. Follow our 8-week plan (see step 4).

STEP 3. Test your progress. Retake the five tests every 4 weeks. If you move up a level, brag to anyone who will listen, then add weight to the strength moves or speed up your cardio. Use the tests as motivation to set personal records in each category. If you're already "strong," or if you completed last year's Fitness Plan, bravo! This workout will help you chart new fitness territory.

STEP 4. Follow the workout online. After you've conquered the first 8 weeks, visit womens healthmag.com/fitplan for the next moves. By signing up, you'll be able to download a new plan every 2 weeks, print moves to take to the gym, watch instructional videos of every exercise, and qualify to win gear and prizes.

TEST NO. 1
Lower-Body Strength

WALL SIT

Stand with your back to a wall, feet hip-width apart. Press your head, shoulders, back, and hips against the wall, then lower your hips until your thighs are parallel to the floor. Hold as long as possible.

Why We Picked It

How long you can literally hold your own weight is the ultimate measure of your muscular endurance—the amount of time your muscles can keep going full force. That's key for everything, from being wobble-free in your favorite Ashtanga class to hauling your new flea market finds upstairs.

WH FIT SCORE

Aspiring 30 to 59 seconds
Solid 1 minute to 1:59
Strong 2:00-plus

TEST NO. 2
Core Strength

HOVER

Get in plank position with your elbows on the floor directly below your shoulders. Hold your body perfectly straight—don't let your back arch or drop—for as long as possible.

Why We Picked It

This move hits your transverse abdominus, one of the muscles that stabilize your core. When your core is weak, your entire body is less stable, putting you at a higher risk for sprains and strains. Beyond that, a brutish middle gives you the power to sprint like a track star or serve like a Wimbledon regular.

WH **FIT SCORE**

Aspiring 20–44 seconds

Solid 45–59 seconds

Strong 1:00-plus

TEST NO. 3
Upper-Body Strength

BALANCE PUSHUP

Get in the bottom of a pushup position with your hands on a stability ball. Keeping your legs and body straight and your feet hip-width apart, balance on your toes. Extend your arms and push your torso off the ball until your arms are nearly straight. Return to starting position and repeat as many times as possible.

Why We Picked It

According to a 2007 study published in the journal *Applied* *Physiology, Nutrition & Metabolism*, placing your hands on a stability ball when doing pushups makes your arms work 30 percent harder than when you have them on the floor.

WH FIT SCORE

Aspiring 1-4 pushups

Solid 5-7 pushups

Strong 8-plus pushups

TEST NO. 4
Balance & Flexibility

STANDING BOW POSE

Stand tall with your feet together and arms at your sides. Lift your right leg and balance on your left. Bend your right knee, then reach back and grasp the inside of your right foot with your right hand. Raise your left arm for balance. Slowly lift your right leg behind you, keeping your hips square and your right knee pointed toward the floor. At the same time, lower your torso, aiming to get as close to parallel to the floor as possible.

Why We Picked It

Talk flexibility and everyone wants to know if you can touch your toes. But it's really the muscles that make up the front of your body—especially your hip flexors and quads—that are the most likely to be as stiff as frozen taffy.

WH FIT SCORE

Aspiring Torso vertical to 45 degrees toward floor
Solid Torso 45 to 90 degrees toward floor
Strong Torso 90 degrees toward floor

TEST NO. 5
Endurance

5-MINUTE RUN

Warm up with a brisk walk for 5 minutes. Then crank up the pace and run as far as you can for 5 minutes. For the easiest scoring, do this on a treadmill.

Why We Picked It

Running is the hallmark of cardio fitness. Duh.

WH **FIT SCORE**

Aspiring 10-minute-mile pace or slower
(½ mile or less)

Solid 8- to 10-minute-mile pace
(more than ½ mile to ⅔ mile)

Strong faster than 8-minute-mile pace
(more than ⅔ mile)

TOTAL FITNESS GUIDE 2009

W|H

CHAPTER EIGHT

ROCK. SOLID. ABS.

THE FIRST INSTALLMENT IN OUR 20-MINUTE WORKOUT SERIES WILL GIVE YOU A BULLETPROOF CORE.

BY JENNY EVERETT

TOTAL FITNESS GUIDE 2009

W|H

YOU'VE BEEN OBSESSING over your abs for almost two decades. That ends now. Because inside this book is a foolproof plan to kick those elusive buggers out of hiding. Finally.

Why's our plan so damn effective? Because it hits your entire core—not just your abs but the muscles that support the spine (see sidebar on page 54)—from all angles with a variety of moves that challenge your stability, balance, and rotational strength. As for results: Do the moves 2 to 3 nonconsecutive days a week and you'll notice a flat-out hot difference in just 30 days.

And here's even better news: Right here you'll find a brand-new workout focused on a different goal—so you can transform your entire body by the end of the year. All of these workouts are designed by WH fitness columnist Amy Dixon, an exercise physiologist and a group fitness manager for Equinox in Santa Monica, California. Apply her genius and marvel at the results.

Bonus Intel! Go to womenshealthmag.com/20minuteworkout to view instructional videos of each move.

CENTER OF ATTENTION

(1) RECTUS ABDOMINUS This muscle—which would (will!) make up your six-pack—runs down the center of your stomach and helps flex your lower spine.

(2) EXTERNAL OBLIQUES These muscles extend from your lower back across the sides of your abdomen. They let you flex your trunk and assist with breathing, especially exhaling.

(3) INTERNAL OBLIQUES These deeper-set muscles let you rotate your torso and bend sideways.

(4) ERECTOR SPINAE These cablelike muscles line the back of your spine and extend up to the base of your skull. They work with your other core muscles to keep your spine stable when you bend and twist.

TRANSVERSE ABDOMINUS Planted deep within the lower half of your abdomen, these muscles stabilize your pelvis. Strengthening them will make you less likely to nosedive when you trip over the edge of your throw rug. Again.

80: Percentage more effort required from your shoulder muscles to hit a tennis ball hard when you have an unstable core

18: Percentage increase in core strength from adding rotational exercises like "walk the plank" (in this book) to your workout

The Core

Challenge your core with these moves twice a week. Do the recommended sets and reps, and, where applicable, opt for a weight that allows you to barely complete the last rep of the final set with perfect form.

WORKOUTS BY AMY DIXON

STABILITY BALL
PELVIC TILT CRUNCH

WORKS CHEST, ABS, HIPS, AND GLUTES

Grab a 5- to 10-pound medicine ball. Lie faceup on a stability ball with back and head pressed into the ball, your feet together on the floor, and the medicine ball positioned against your chest (A). Brace your abs and crunch up until your shoulders are off the ball. Then reach the ball toward the ceiling (B). That's 1 rep. Do 3 sets of 12 to 15 reps, resting for 30 seconds between each set.

A

B

WALK THE PLANK AND ROTATE

WORKS ENTIRE CORE, SHOULDERS, CHEST, BACK, AND HIPS

Get in plank position with your hands on a 12- to 18-inch step (A). With your weight on your left arm, rotate your body while raising your right arm toward the ceiling (B). Return to plank position and step your right arm down to the right of the bench, then your left arm down to the left of the bench. Step back up, leading with your left arm. That's 1 rep. Do 8 to 10 reps, rest for 30 seconds, then repeat, twisting to the opposite side.

Trainer Tip

Mastered this move? Make it even more challenging by stacking your feet in the side plank position.

A

B

STIFF-LEG
PULLOVER CRUNCH

WORKS UPPER BACK, ABS, AND HIPS

Grab a pair of 10- to 12-pound dumbbells and lie on your back with your arms behind you. Extend your legs at a 45-degree angle (A). Bring your arms up over your chest and lift your shoulders off the mat while raising your legs until they're perpendicular to the floor (B). Return to start (don't let your legs touch the floor). That's 1 rep. Do 3 sets of 15 reps, resting for 30 seconds between sets.

A

B

THE MATRIX

WORKS ABS, BACK, GLUTES, AND QUADS

Grab a 5- to 10-pound medicine ball and kneel on the floor with your knees hip-width apart. Lengthen your spine and press the ball against your abs (A). Slowly lean back as far as possible, keeping your knees planted (B). Hold the reclined position for 3 seconds, then use your core to slowly come up to the starting position. That's 1 rep. Do 3 sets of 15 reps, resting for 30 seconds between sets.

Trainer Tip

When coming back up, brace your core, resist using momentum, and keep your head and neck in line with your spine.

A

B

KNEE-TO-CHEST CRUNCH

WORKS ENTIRE CORE, SHOULDERS, CHEST,
HIPS, AND GLUTES

Get in plank position with your hands shoulder-width
apart on a stability ball (A). Draw your right knee
toward your chest (B). Hold for 1 second, then return
to plank position. That's 1 rep. Do 12 to 15 reps. Rest
for 30 seconds, then repeat with the other leg.

A

B

W|H

PRONE OBLIQUE ROLL

WORKS SHOULDERS, CHEST, OBLIQUES, BACK, AND GLUTES

Get in plank position with your shins about hip-width apart on a stability ball and your hands shoulder-width apart on the floor (A). Keeping your feet on the ball, draw your right knee toward your right shoulder (the left just comes along for the ride) (B). Return to center. Do 12 to 15 reps, rest for 30 seconds, then repeat to the other side.

Trainer Tip

As you draw your knees across your body, focus on rotating your core and activating your obliques. To help with balance, pick one spot on the floor and stare at it.

A

B

REAR LEG RAISE

WORKS LOWER BACK AND GLUTES

Rest your hips and stomach on a stability ball. Straighten your legs and position your toes hip-width apart on the floor. Extend your arms in line with your shoulders (A). Lift your right leg about 6 inches off of the floor while reaching your arms as far out as possible (B). That's 1 rep. Do 15 reps, then repeat to the other side without resting between sets.

A

B

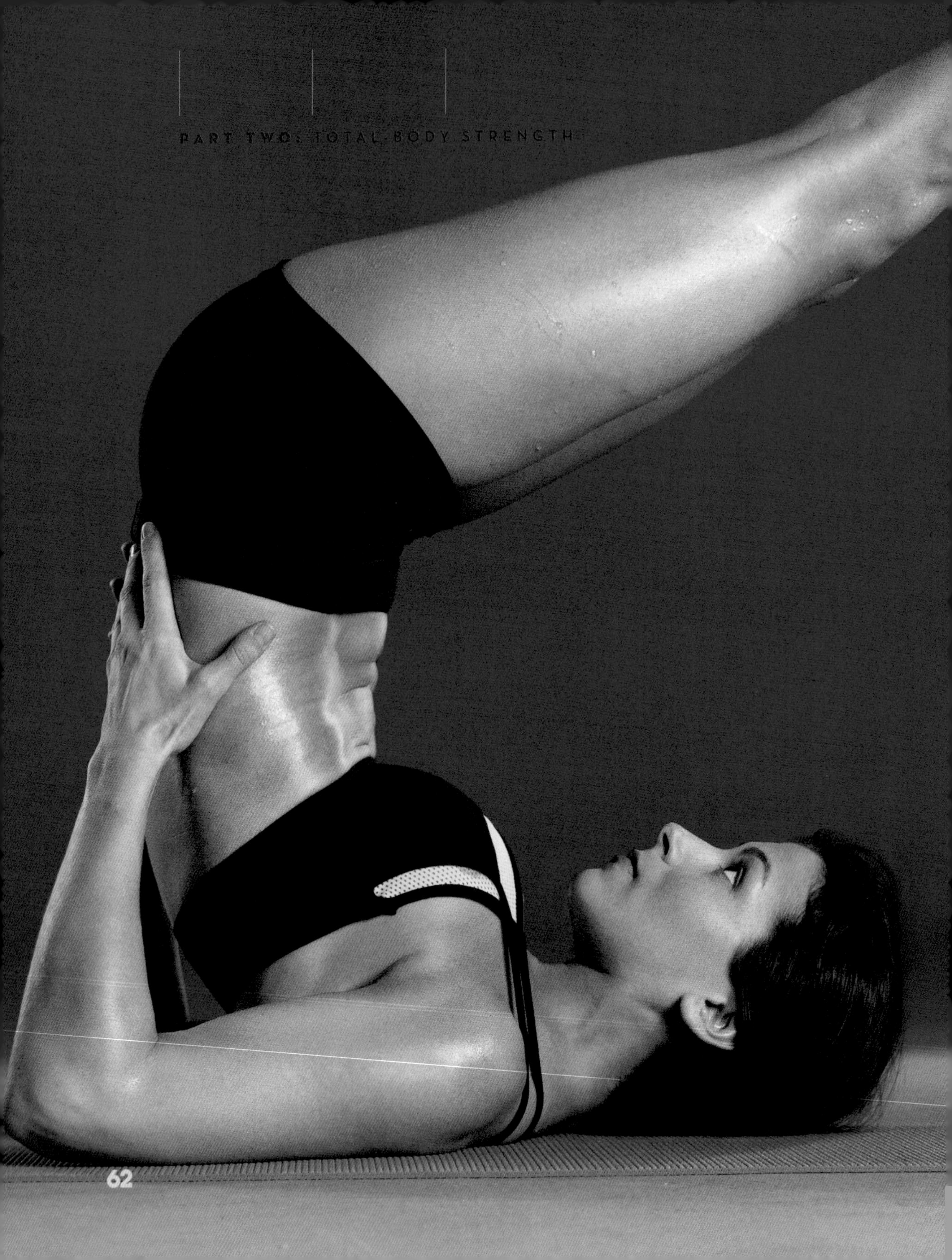

CHAPTER NINE

WE'VE GOT YOU COVERED

DON'T MISS A SINGLE MUSCLE WITH OUR 20-MINUTE WORKOUT SERIES.

BY JENNY EVERETT

IF YOU WANT A BODY that works as great as it looks (and vice versa), this total-body routine is the answer. You'll not only hit max muscle, which ups your metabolism, but also strengthen your core and hone your balance to protect injury-prone spots. Tackle the moves from *WH* columnist Amy Dixon, an exercise physiologist and group fitness manager for Equinox in Santa Monica, California, two nonconsecutive days a week and you'll be a well-rounded (not round!) fitness specimen.

Row for It

If you don't want to deal with weights and whatnot, turn to a 20-minute workout on the rowing machine—it's a multitasking calorie killer extraordinaire. To be sure you hit the most muscle possible, follow these pointers from three-time Olympic rower Judy Geer.

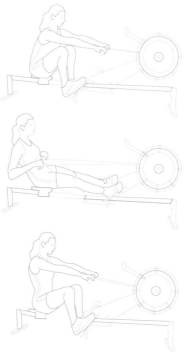

Start

Sit on the seat with your knees bent enough that your shins are perpendicular to the floor. Bend forward at the hips and grab the handles.

Finish

Extend your legs and press your heels into the footrest to engage your upper legs. Lean back slightly and pull your hands to your chest.

Recover

Straighten your arms, lean your torso forward, and gradually bend your legs to slide the seat forward until you reach the starting position.

Tone Zone

For a head-to-toe hard body, do these moves twice a week. Where applicable, opt for a weight at which you can barely eke out the last rep of your final set with perfect form.

WORKOUTS BY AMY DIXON

TEST THE WATER

WORKS BICEPS AND ENTIRE LOWER BODY

Grab a pair of 8- to 10-pound dumbbells and stand on a 1- to 2-foot-high step or bench with your feet together and your arms at your sides with palms facing forward. Lift your right foot off the bench (A) and squat down a few inches. Press back up and curl the dumbbells up to your shoulders (B). That's one rep. Do three sets of 12 to 15, then repeat on the other side. Rest for 30 seconds between sets.

Trainer Tip

Keep your elbows tight against your torso as you curl the dumbbells.

A

B

TAKE A WALK

WORKS TRICEPS AND CORE

Place a BOSU on the floor and sit on the dome's
center. Place your palms on the ball alongside your
hips with your fingertips facing forward, and place
your heels on the floor about 2 feet from the base of
the BOSU. Straighten your arms and lift your hips off
the ball (A). Lift both your right hand and your left foot
a few inches (B). Hold for 1 second, then lower and
repeat with the other hand and foot. That's one rep.
Do three sets of 15 to 20, resting for 30 seconds
between sets.

A

B

CHAPTER TEN

TUNE IN TO CABLE

YOUR PERFECT BODY COMES DOWN TO THE WIRE.

WHILE SUCKED INTO ANOTHER EPISODE of *MythBusters*, you wonder: What did I do before cable? Soon you'll be asking the same question at the gym—about the cable-pulley machine. That hulking object is probably your gym's best-kept secret because its flexible cables work your muscles in every direction. You also hit your core by fighting the momentum that pulls you back toward the machine. Get a full-body fix in 15 minutes with these moves from Jonathan Sexsmith, C.S.C.S., a personal trainer in New York City. Choose a weight that lets you complete the reps with perfect form.

CABLE JOG

WORKS ENTIRE BODY, ESPECIALLY THE CORE, GLUTES, AND LEGS

Set two cables at shoulder height. Grab a handle in each hand and stand about a foot from the machine with your back to it. Position the handles on either side of your chest, palms facing each other, then walk forward until there's no slack in the cable. Jog forward three or four strides, and then jog back. Continue for 30 seconds. That's one set. Do three.

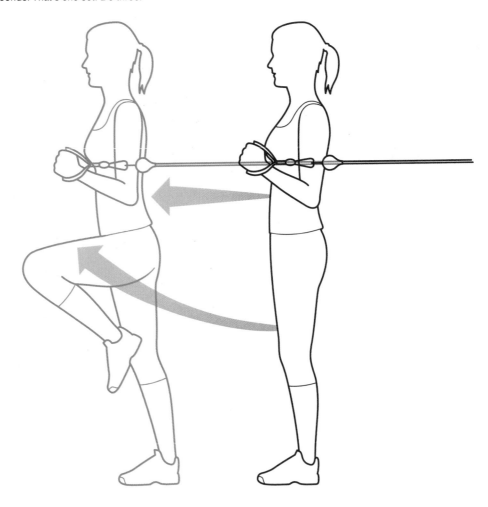

LUNGE AND PRESS

WORKS TRICEPS, CHEST, ABS, GLUTES,
HAMSTRINGS, AND QUADS

Position a cable so it will be at shoulder level when
you lunge. Grab the cable's handle with your left hand
and face away from the machine. With the handle
next to your chest, take a giant step back with your
left foot and lower your hips. At the same time, press
the cable straight out at shoulder height. Do three
sets of 10 reps on each side.

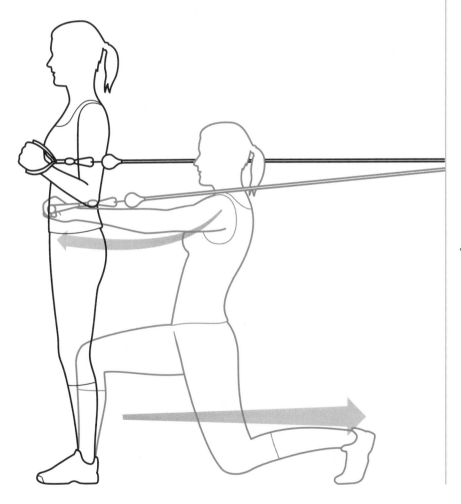

W|H

SWORD DRAW

WORKS SHOULDERS, BACK, ABS, GLUTES,
AND HAMSTRINGS

Position a cable at the lowest level. Facing the
machine, hold the cable in your right hand. Step back
to remove any slack in the cable. Take a giant step
back with your right leg and sink into a lunge until your
left thigh is parallel to the floor. Keeping your arm
straight, pull the cable out to your right until your hand
is at eye level while raising your right knee to hip level
as you return to standing. That's 1 rep. Do three sets
of 8 reps on each side.

CABLE ARCHER

WORKS BICEPS, BACK, GLUTES,
AND HAMSTRINGS

Position one cable so it's at shoulder height. Place
your left hand on your hip and grab the cable's handle
with your right hand. Step back so there's tension
when your arm is straight out in front of you. Facing
the machine, step back with the right foot to 7 o'clock.
At the same time, pull your right hand toward you
archery-style until it reaches the right side of your
chest. Return to start by stepping your right foot back
in and straightening your right arm. Do three sets of
10 reps on each side.

W|H

food rules

Fueling your body for everything from workouts to your day at the office can be a daunting enterprise. Here you'll find useful advice for avoiding fad diets, beating stress with food, controlling portions, and fighting cravings. In no time, you'll be a whiz at decoding your diet for every activity in your busy schedule.

DIET FOOD
====

TASTES LIKE

HELL

AND TO HELL
IT SHALL RETURN
==

1930-2008

CHAPTER ELEVEN

DIET'S DEMISE

GOOD RIDDANCE TO FAD DIETS AND FAKE FOOD—THERE ARE BETTER WAYS TO LOSE YOUR JIGGLY BITS.

BY JILL WALDBIESER, ADDITIONAL REPORTING BY AMY PATUREL, M.S., M.P.H.

DIET FOODS AND FADS: We knew you, but we didn't love you. Call us heartless, but we're happy to see you go. We could tell the end was near when we started seeing headlines like "Fad Diets Less Popular Today Than Five Years Ago" and when Weight Watchers kicked off its 2008 ad campaign, "Stop dieting. Start living." According to the Calorie Control Council (CCC), an international nonprofit representing the low-calorie and reduced-fat food and beverage industry, die-hard dieting has seen its last days—the number of Americans on restrictive meal plans, according to the CCC's national survey, has dropped from 20 percent to 13 percent

since 2004, and the word *diet* is one of the least-preferred terms on nutrition labels. "Diet has a very negative connotation," says Beth Hubrich, R.D., the CCC's executive director. Now that we've wised up to the fact that there's no magical way to thinner thighs, we can say good riddance to meals that taste like the box they come in and march into bikini season with a smarter, more successful strategy for shaking off our belly jiggle once and for all.

American History XXL

Food gimmicks and fad diets may seem as if they were spawned by Satan himself, but as far as we can tell, mere mortals are the ones to blame. The first diet book came out of London in 1864: William Banting's *A Letter on Corpulence* promoted a punitive diet of lean meats and dry toast. The first known weight-loss product was cooked up a few decades later, in 1930, in the back of an American beauty parlor: Dr. Stoll's Diet Aid, a combo of milk chocolate, starch, and an extract of roasted wheat and bran. Setting a precedent for the thousands of diet products to follow, it failed to deliver.

But the diet industry didn't truly explode until the 1980s, when several studies shifted the focus from food itself to specific components—specifically, fat, sugar, and salt. Store shelves suddenly began to spill over with fat-free, sugar-free, and low-sodium versions of favorite foods promising to help the average American girl achieve Olivia Newton-John's sticklike figure. Ironically, many of these products contained preservatives or, in the case of fat-free offerings, extra sugar, making them no less fattening than regular food. "We used to think noncaloric sweeteners were going to be the panacea that would save all of America," says James Painter, Ph.D., chair of the School of Family and Consumer Sciences at Eastern Illinois University. "But during the same period that they started being used in products, obesity was doubling in this country."

The Great "Lite" Hype

It doesn't take Alan Greenspan to decipher the cause of Americans' waist inflation. We simply have too much fattening food available all the time. "Thirty, 40 years ago, you couldn't find places where you could get food in one minute," Painter says. "Now you have to go past 1,000 drive-thrus just to buy your gas. Because we can eat whenever we want, we overeat." The antidote, until recently, has been to suddenly and severely change our eating habits to lose weight quickly—in other words, go on a diet. But here's why that strategy belongs 6 feet under: **It screws with our minds.**

Over the past 15 years, the number of restaurants and stores offering diet options has increased dramatically—a change that has done more harm than good. A 2006 study published in the *Journal of Marketing Research* found that we eat more calories when a food is labeled low-fat, probably because we don't experience the guilt that would otherwise make us put on the brakes mid-binge. "People think, 'Oh, this is sugar-free or fat-free, so I can eat as much as I want,'" Painter says. Filling up on these foods (and on hope) only to end up heavier than before can be dejecting, so it's understandable that chronic dieting is linked with depression, low self-esteem, and increased stress. **We can't stick with it.**

Diets do work—while you're on them. But up to two-thirds of dieters end up heavier after 5 years than when they started out. And in clinical studies, the more time that passes between the end of a subject's diet and the time she's reassessed, the more weight she will have regained. The most likely reason for the rebound is that as soon as dieters stop following a strict set of rules (no eating after 7 p.m., no snacking between meals . . .), they lapse into the same habits that made them gain weight in the first place. **Our bodies rebel.**

Depriving yourself in this way can slow your metabolism to a snail's pace and make losing weight even harder. "Once your body realizes it's not getting as much food, it starts to conserve energy," Painter says. Thanks to evolution, your inner cave girl is fattening up for what she thinks could be another ice age. Continue to starve yourself and you'll suffer from intense cravings and loss of lean body tissue, aka muscle; that further compromises your body's ability to burn calories. **We have a need for speed.**

Getting results fast is the American way, but losing more than 1 or 2 pounds a week is self-sabotage. Researchers have discovered that leptin, a hormone secreted by fat cells, helps control appetite by binding to receptors in the brain to tell you you're full. But leptin and fat are a package deal: Lose fat and you lose leptin, too. "When leptin levels are low, the body reacts by conserving energy expenditure so much that you stop burning calories at a normal rate," says Andrea Giancoli, M.

P.H., R.D., national spokesperson for the American Dietetic Association. "And that triggers weight regain."

Weight Loss Reborn

As satisfying as it feels to kick the restrictive, taste-deficient, fat-obsessed plans of the past out the door, the last thing we want to do is check ourselves into the DoubleChin Hotel for life. The average adult gains about one and a half pounds every year after age 30, says John Foreyt, Ph.D., a professor of medicine and the director of the Behavioral Medicine Research Center at Baylor College of Medicine in Houston. But even if their personal trainer looks like Matthew Fox, most women can't spend 2 or more hours a day at the gym. So how do we take a bite out of our bloat? The key, experts say, is the opposite of quick fixes

and trick foods: small, gradual, healthy, permanent changes.

THINK FOREVER "If you can't see yourself eating or exercising a certain way for the rest of your life—say, consuming raw food and running 5 miles every day—you shouldn't be doing it to lose weight in the first place," says Linda Spangle, R.N., M.A., author of *100 Days of Weight Loss*. The only changes that work are those you can continue indefinitely. If you reach your goal weight when you're hitting the gym three times a week and cooking your own meals instead of getting takeout—and those are changes you know you can live with—then they're going to work a whole lot better than any short-term shtick. "Weight management has to be an uncompromising, non-negotiable, everyday thing, like brushing your teeth," Spangle says.

THINK SMALL Before you revamp your eating habits, take a few weeks to write down everything you eat, Painter says. "Don't count fat, protein, calories, portions—just keep track of what you've already consumed before you put the next thing in your mouth. It gives your brain a chance to say no." Once you see it all on paper, look for small, simple ways to scale back. It's easier than you think: Switch from a roast beef sandwich on a bun with provolone and mayo to roast beef in a whole-wheat pita with light Swiss and mustard. Instead of eating cocktail peanuts, munch on pistachios that you have to peel one by one. "These small-scale techniques sound insignificant, but they are the answers we're all looking for," he says.

THINK PHYSICAL It's called the "French Paradox": the totally unfair way Parisian women linger over multicourse, très riches dinners, drink all the wine they want, and have dessert, yet still look great in their La Perla. The reason: Studies show that the French rely more on internal cues (like when they're comfortably full) and Americans rely on external cues (like when D*esperate Housewives* ends). "We're not paying attention to what we eat or how much," Spangle says, "and often, not even to whether we're really physically hungry. People eat for social reasons, or because they've had a bad day, or for comfort." To retrain yourself to heed hunger cues, imagine your stomach as a gas tank. After every bite, check in to see where the dial is hovering. Close to empty? Right in the middle? Learn to never let it push past full.

THINK ACTION In an ongoing study of dieters who maintained a weight loss of 30 pounds for at least one year, 90 percent report that regular physical exercise is the key to sustaining their loss. And a study conducted at Baylor College of Medicine suggests that diet and exercise are more effective for losing and maintaining weight than diet alone. Researchers assigned 127 subjects to one of three interventions for one year: diet only, exercise only, or diet plus exercise. All participants lost similar

amounts of weight in the first year, but when they were reassessed during year two, the diet-only crew gained 2 pounds over the weight they started at, while the groups that included exercise remained 5 pounds below. An exercise routine may be a bitch to start, but thanks to the happy-hormone rush we get when we break a sweat, it can quickly become a healthy addiction.

Sure, taking off the extra flab is more work than putting it on probably was, but even when the going gets tough, it's better than eating nothing but cabbage soup, avoiding the bread aisle, or choking down food you hate. "People no longer have to make themselves miserable in order to lose weight," Spangle says. In other words, dieting may be dead, but your beach-ready bod will live on.

CHAPTER TWELVE

EAT TO BEAT
STRESS

NINE FOODS THAT'LL KEEP YOU JOLLY DURING THE HELL-IDAYS

BY MORGAN LORD

TOTAL FITNESS GUIDE 2009

W|H

FORGET EVERYTHING YOU'VE HEARD about stress-eating being a bad thing. If you put the right foods in your piehole (i.e., not pie), noshing when your nerves are jangling more than the bells on Santa's sleigh can actually calm you down. And that's great news, because the last thing you need is more stress, which over time can increase your risk of high blood pressure, heart disease, and obesity— and the odds that you'll go ballistic on Mom when she asks, for the third time, what your unemployed fiancé does for a living. These yummy, easy-to-find foods soothe stress and can counteract the damage that chronic pressure does to your bod. Stock up on the lot of them so that when the tension rises along with the temperature in Grandma's kitchen, you can eat instead of freak.

Almonds, Pistachios & Walnuts

When all hell breaks loose, reach for a handful of almonds. They're bursting with vitamin E, an antioxidant that bolsters the immune system. Almonds also contain B vitamins, which may help your body hold up during seriously unpleasant events (like

getting a year's membership to Match.com as a present). About a quarter cup every day is all you need. Another easy way to get a fix is to switch from traditional PB to almond butter on high-tension days. (We like All Natural Barney Butter Almond Butter, $7, barneybutter.com.)

Sick of almonds? Shell pistachios or crack walnuts. Both will help keep your heart from racing when things heat up. "We experience immediate cardiovascular responses to stress because of the 'fight or flight' response," says Sheila G. West, M.D., associate professor of biobehavioral health at Penn State. When stress strikes, the hormone adrenaline raises blood pressure to boost energy—so you're prepared to run like hell if you need to. But because we seldom need to fight or flee (dodging your annoying aunt doesn't count), it's better to blunt the strain on your heart. A 2007 Penn State study led by Dr. West found that eating one and a half ounces (about a handful) of pistachios a day lowers blood pressure so your heart doesn't have to work overtime. Walnuts have also been found to lower blood pressure, both at rest and under stress, West says. Add about an ounce to salads, cereal, or oatmeal.

Avocados

The next time stress has you hankering for a high-fat, creamy treat, skip the ice cream and try some homemade guacamole—the thick, rich texture can satisfy your craving and reduce those frantic feelings. Plus, the green wonders' double whammy of monounsaturated fat and potassium can lower blood pressure. One of the best ways to reduce high blood pressure, according to the National Heart, Lung, and Blood Institute, is to get enough potassium—and just half an avocado offers 487 milligrams, more than you'll get from a medium-size banana. To whip up your own avocado salad dressing, purée a medium avocado with 2 tablespoons of lemon juice and a dash of cayenne.

Skim Milk

Science backs up the old warm-milk remedy for insomnia and restlessness. Turns out calcium can reduce muscle spasms and soothe tension, says Mary Dallman, Ph.D., professor of physiology at the University of California, San Francisco. A glass of moo juice (preferably skim or 1 percent) may also reduce stressful PMS symptoms such as mood swings, anxiety, and irritability. According to a 2005 study from the Archives of Internal Medicine, women who drank four or more servings of low-fat or skim milk per day had a 46 percent lower risk of pre-period misery than women who had no more than one serving per week.

Oatmeal

Carbohydrates make the brain produce more serotonin, the same relaxing brain chemical released when you eat dark chocolate. The more slowly your body absorbs carbs, the more steadily serotonin flows, according to Judith Wurtman, Ph.D., a former MIT research scientist and co-author of *The Serotonin Power Diet*. The result: a less-likely-to-snap you. Because thick, hearty oatmeal is high in fiber, few things take longer for your stomach to digest, says Elizabeth Somer, M.A., R.D., author of *Food & Mood*. Wurtman also recommends topping it with a swirl of jam for a quicker release of serotonin. When you know it's

going to be a doozy of a day, avoid heavily processed varieties (e.g., the sugary kind that comes in packets meant for the microwave), which are digested more quickly, and take the time to make thick-cut old-fashioned oats, like McCann's Original Steel-Cut Irish Oatmeal ($6 for 28 oz, amazon.com). But if two minutes for breakfast is all you have, you can still do your mood a favor by opting for instant oatmeal over Cocoa Puffs.

Oranges

Fretting over a job interview or presentation at work? Pour yourself a glass of Florida's famous juice or peel yourself an orange. The magic nutrient here is vitamin C. In a study in *Psychopharmacology*, German researchers subjected 120

W|H

people to a public-speaking task plus a series of math problems. Those who took 3,000 milligrams of vitamin C reported that they felt less stressed, and their blood pressure and levels of cortisol (a stress hormone) returned to normal faster. "Vitamin C is also a well-known immune system booster," says Amy Jamieson-Petonic, R.D., a spokesperson for the American Dietetic Association. So don't be bummed that you got a fruit-of-the-month-club gift instead of the video iPOD—you're going to need all those oranges and grapefruits.

Salmon

Stress hormones have an archenemy: omega-3 fatty acids. A 2003 study from *Diabetes & Metabolism* found that a diet rich in omega-3 fatty acids kept cortisol and adrenaline from geysering. Omega-3 fatty acids also protect against heart disease, according to a 2002 study in the *Journal of the American Medical Association*. "Eat a 3-ounce serving of fish, especially fatty fish like salmon, mackerel, herring, and light tuna, at least twice a week," Jamieson-Petonic says. Not a fish eater? For another omega-3 punch, buy foods fortified with DHA (you'll find this particular fatty acid in eggs, yogurt, milk, and soy products); but don't go out of your way for products that boast

booming levels of ALA, another fatty acid, which may not work as well.

Spinach

Magnesium was made to calm holiday insanity. First, the mineral can help lower your stress levels, keeping your body in a state of relative ease as you kick off yet another round of small talk at the company party. Not getting enough magnesium may trigger migraine headaches and make you feel fatigued. (And almost seven out of 10 of us don't get enough of the stuff. No wonder we're cranky.) Just one cup of spinach provides 40 percent of your daily value—so try subbing it for lettuce on sandwiches and salads. (And now you have an excuse to indulge in the spinach dip!)

STRESS-BUSTING MEAL PLAN

MORNING

Mellow Menu

BREAKFAST: Top plain oatmeal with slivered almonds (a golf ball–size serving), dried cranberries (dried fruit offers all the health benefits of regular fruit), and a splash of DHA-fortified low-fat milk. Wash it down with an 8-ounce glass of Tropicana Healthy Heart with Omega-3 orange juice.

SNACK: Munch on pistachio popcorn to satisfy sweet, salty, and nutty cravings: Top a Pop Secret 100 Calorie Pop pack with 2 tablespoons of shelled pistachios and a sprinkling of vanilla extract.

AFTERNOON

Mellow Menu

LUNCH: Build your own stress-battling BLT—toast whole wheat bread and stack on about a cup of spinach, a strip or two of crispy turkey bacon, and tomato slices. To drink, have an iced OJ spritzer (half orange juice, half sparkling mineral water).

SNACK: Toast a Kellogg's Eggo Nutri-Grain Low Fat Whole Wheat waffle and top it with a tablespoon of almond butter.

EVENING

Mellow Menu

DINNER: Have grilled salmon topped with avocado-tomato salsa (add a quarter of an

avocado, cubed, to your favorite salsa) on a bed of fresh spinach.

SNACK: Indulge in three squares of an Endangered Species Chocolate Dark Chocolate with Blueberries bar and a glass of low-fat milk. ($3.15, chocolatebar.com)

CHAPTER THIRTEEN

CRAVING
MAD

OUTSMART ANY URGE WITH THESE STICK-TO-YOUR-DIET TRICKS.

BY JUDI KETTELER

IF, IN THE NEXT 30 SECONDS, you don't think about a gooey slab of warm chocolate cake, Evan Forman, assistant professor of psychology at Drexel University, will mail you a check for a million dollars. Forman loves to pose this mind-screw to his study subjects because he knows that thoughts are like zits—they pop up whether you want them to or not. And that's the problem with cravings. "While there are things you can do to manage cravings, you can't stop yourself from thinking about the foods you love," Forman says.

Unlike run-of-the-mill hunger, cravings—intense desires for certain

foods—seem to be linked to our brain's reward system. Emotions, situations, or pleasant associations (Grandma fed you Little Debbie snack cakes) can trigger a craving, says Susan Roberts, Ph.D., director of the Energy Metabolism Laboratory at the Tufts University Jean Mayer USDA Human Nutrition Research Center on Aging. When you eat a food you crave, your brain releases dopamine, a natural chemical related to pleasure. It's the same reward system you get from sex or illegal drugs, "but it's at much lower concentrations," Roberts says.

So what to do the next time you start jonesing for a pumpkin spice latte when you're already stuffed from lunch? The following stay-slim strategies will boost your ability to just say no.

Craving Killer No. 1

Accept Defeat

Playing head games isn't the only way Forman and his colleagues torture dieters in the name of science. They gave 98 study participants a questionnaire to determine how susceptible they were to food urges, then loaded them up with transparent boxes of Hershey's Kisses they had to keep with them at all times for the next 48 hours. Those who proved most successful at fighting temptation used an acceptance-based strategy they had been taught: Acknowledge the craving, accept it, and choose not to act on it. When you're struck by the desire for that double-fudge cake, practice what Forman calls cognitive "defusion": Instead of trying to ignore the craving, admit to yourself that you want a slice. It works on the same principle as getting the hots for a co-worker when you're in a great relationship: Recognizing that you'll always be attracted to cute guys (or yummy food) prevents you from acting on the feeling every time it comes up.

Craving Killer No. 2

Give in—a Little

Now this is our kind of news: Recent research from Tufts University revealed that surrendering to a craving is sometimes the best course of action—as long as you can practice portion control. In a study of 32 overweight women, all averaged an 8 percent weight loss after 12 months, but those who were most successful gave in to their cravings occasionally. When they did indulge, they ate small amounts—just enough to be satisfied, says Roberts, one of the study's co-authors. The key is practicing restraint, not deprivation. "When you forbid a food, it only becomes more attractive, and you become likely to overeat," says Janet Polivy, Ph.D.,

professor of psychology at the University of Toronto. So when you need to feed the cocoa monster, reach for a prepackaged snack, such as Entenmann's Little Bites 100 Calorie Pack Brownie Squares, and call it a day. You'll be much less likely to break down and attack an entire hot fudge sundae.

Craving Killer No. 3

Fantasize

Being told to think of something else when you're in the grip of a powerful craving is about as helpful as being told to swim when you're drowning. But

there is one way that advice can work: Researchers at Flinders University in Australia found that occupying your senses with a vivid nonfood fantasy just might stifle your urge.

"Your short-term memory has limited storage," says study author Eva Kemps. To conjure any image—nachos or that spring break in Cancun—you need to pull them out of your long-term memory, the way an iPod cues up one song at a time from the gazillion it has in storage. But short-term memory has only so much room; it can't play "Cheeseburger in Paradise" and "Holiday" at the same time. "The idea is to keep your short-term memory busy by fantasizing about something else," Kemps says.

It worked for Kemps's study participants. When they were asked to drum up remembered smells and sights—the scent of freshly cut grass or a log fire, and images such as a hot-air balloon or the Sydney Opera House—their cravings for chocolate (which was right in front of them) were reduced by about 30 percent. Their minds couldn't handle the craving and the new sensory imagery at the same time, so the craving got dumped. Try thinking about what your guy looks like in nothing but a towel—you might forget all about that cookie.

Craving Killer No. 4

Swap Smart

No one has ever made a longing for a jelly doughnut disappear by gnawing on celery sticks. But that doesn't mean substitutions never work. It's all about satisfying your appetite. The secret, Roberts

THINK ABOUT YOUR GUY IN NOTHING BUT A TOWEL—YOU'LL FORGET THAT COOKIE.

DIVIDE AND CONQUER

If you can resist a craving for 20 minutes, it might be gone for good. Here are 10 ways to wait it out.

UPDATE YOUR SHOPPING AND WISH LISTS at Amazon.com and Target.com.

DIY MANICURE. Wet nails can't reach into a chip bag. If the craving lingers, recoat.

LOOK THROUGH YOUR PHOTO ALBUM. As you walk down memory lane, flip to a photo of you looking smokin' hot.

BRUSH AND FLOSS YOUR TEETH. The minty freshness is sure to ruin dessert.

HAVE SEX. Let a hot quickie drive you to distraction.

TAKE A BUBBLE BATH. Suds and cookie crumbs don't mix.

READ A GOSSIP MAGAZINE. Gawking at the mug shot of the celeb you love to hate can help you police food crimes.

DOWNLOAD A SONG. Spend your vending-machine money on music instead, and you'll fill out your iPod, not your thighs.

CALL A FRIEND. Recruit a craving buddy and call each other when you're on the verge.

ORGANIZE A CLOTHES DRAWER. Remind yourself how much you love that pair of pants—just the size they are.

says, is to get the flavor you want with minimal caloric damage. If you can't stop thinking about caramel corn, try LesserEvil "SinNamon" kettle corn (one cup has about 120 calories and 2 grams of fat). Or, give in to a sweet tooth with fruit—natural sugar can be amazingly satisfying. "Sometimes you have to reinvent a sweet," says Cheryl Forberg, R.D., nutritionist for the TV show *The Biggest Loser*. Try frozen grapes instead of popsicles and fresh cherries instead of candy.

One caveat: When it comes to chocolate (one of the most-craved foods in the world), it's better not to accept imitations. A study from the University of Toronto found that chronic dieters didn't have as much trouble resisting vanilla as they did chocolate. The reason, Polivy says, may be that although vanilla cravings may be sated by other flavors, like cinnamon or butterscotch, chocolate is unique—nothing else seems to hit the spot.

When you do indulge, keep an eye on how much. Get your fix in small (about 150-calorie) doses—that's two chocolate truffles or one snack-size chocolate bar. And don't tempt yourself by keeping supersize chocolate bars and trays of brownies at the ready—we already know who'll win that bet.

8 Shrimp and 4 Tablespoons Cocktail Sauce

The perfect appetizer—and no one at the table will know you're counting calories.

CHAPTER FOURTEEN

PORTION
PATROL

SCORE MAXIMUM SATISFACTION FROM 100 CALORIES
WITH THESE 28 SNACKS.

BY LISA DRAYER, R.D.

COMPUTER SCREENS, DOGS, YOUR PAYCHECK: Some things should only come in size XL. But at snack time, smaller really is better. A mere 100 calories can satisfy you until your next meal, but that amount is frustratingly hard to eyeball. You could pay the more than 100 percent markup some companies charge for 100-cal snack packs—or simply keep these delish, nutritionist-approved treats on hand.

Starbucks Tall Skinny Latte

Score your caffeine fix along with a hunger-crushing 10-gram shot of protein and about a third of your daily calcium needs.

Sprinkle of Feta and Olive Oil

Lunch left something to be desired? This savory dish will make your taste buds happy.

Vitamuffin VitaTop

Pop this vitamin-rich fudgy treat before a morning meeting and that Danish won't look so damn good.

Banana

Naturally prepackaged goodness you can take anywhere, with the added benefit of cramp-preventing potassium.

½ Cup Edamame (measured shelled)

Eating this protein-packed pick-me-up out of the shell will help make the snack last longer.

Quaker Instant Oatmeal (regular flavor)

This speedy fiber- and protein-packed breakfast also makes for a warm, filling snack.

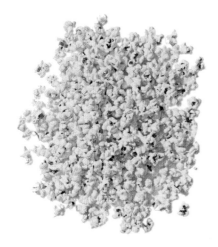

3 Cups Air-Popped Popcorn

Go ahead, nibble mindlessly as you zone out in front of Bravo. Even if you're watching trash, you won't be eating it.

Yoplait Light Yogurt (fruit flavors)

This bone-building goodie provides 20 percent of your RDA for calcium and vitamin D.

DUMB QUESTION:

WHAT'S A CALORIE?

Scientifically speaking, it's the amount of energy needed to raise the temperature of 1 gram of water by one degree Celsius. Nutritionally, a calorie is the amount of energy in food your body can use. Digestion releases nutrients in food, which your body converts to glucose and uses to fuel all of its functions, from making your heart beat to running after the UPS truck. We can thank (or curse) Lulu Hunt Peters for introducing the concept of counting calories. Her 1918 bestseller, *Diet and Health With Key to the Calories*, advocated the "calories in, calories out" method as a way to regulate weight. We've been adding them up ever since.

Curves Granola Bar

Stash chocolate-peanut or strawberries-and-cream bars in your glove box to help you resist the lure of the drive-thru when you're on the road.

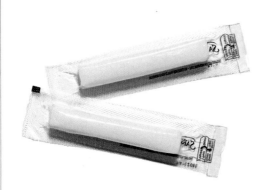

2 Sargento Light String Cheese Snacks

Any food you can play with is a great distraction; plus, the protein battles mid-afternoon hunger pangs.

1 Cup Baby Carrots with 2 Tablespoons Hummus

The crunchy texture keeps choppers busy, and tangy hummus feeds your need for comfort food.

1¼ Ounces Turkey Jerky

When you must have meat, chew on this low-cal, low-fat power snack.

½ Cantaloupe

Like most fruit, melon contains a lot of water. So you get a lot of food—and beta-carotene—for not a lot of calories.

1 Cup Vegetable Juice, such as V8, and 2 Ounces Oscar Mayer Oven-Roasted Turkey Breast

An antioxidant- and protein-rich hunger-buster.

1 Tablespoon Peanuts and 2 Tablespoons Dried Cranberries

Toss together this pared-down trail mix and pre-measure into plastic baggies.

1 Cup Strawberries and 3 Tablespoons Cool Whip Free

For a totally guiltless dessert, dish up a bowl of this sweet, fiber-rich combo.

1 Cup Raspberries with 2 Tablespoons Plain Yogurt and 1 Tablespoon Honey

This sweet mix does the job until you can break away from your desk for a full meal.

3 Amy's Cheese Pizza Snacks

These hot, crispy, cheesy bites are possibly the most satisfying late-night snack ever.

2 Egg Whites with 1 Slice Whole Wheat Toast

This protein-and-carb duo gives you a light but energizing start when you have a belly-busting lunch on your calendar.

About ½ Cup Frozen Yogurt

When you crave a cool treat, dip into smooth and yummy fro-yo—it's nowhere near as high-calorie as ice cream.

⅔ Cup Barbara's Bakery Cinnamon Puffins Cereal (dry)

Keep premeasured tubs in your desk drawer for an alternative to kettle chips when you're craving something crunchy.

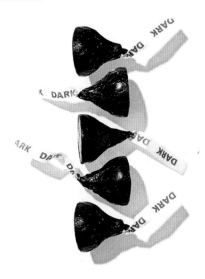

5 Hershey's Special Dark Chocolate Kisses

A cocoa fix that's equally rich in chocolaty taste and disease-fighting antioxidants—what more could you want in a snack?

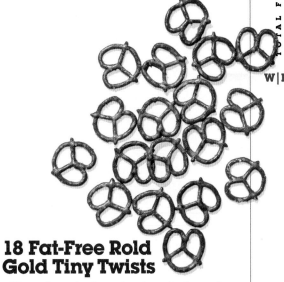

18 Fat-Free Rold Gold Tiny Twists

Kill a carbs-and-salt craving in a single snack session.

1 Ounce Yellowtail and 1 Ounce Tuna Sashimi with 1 Packet Kikkoman Instant Tofu Miso Soup

Have it pre-party: The protein will keep you from wiping out the buffet.

Chocolate Milk (1 Cup nonfat milk + 1 Tablespoon Hershey's Lite chocolate syrup)

Quell your inner cocoa monster and get a hit of calcium.

2 Ounce Veggie Land Veg-T-Balls with 2 Tablespoons Muir Glen Chunky Tomato Sauce

These low-fat vegetarian balls hit the spot.

1 Nutter Butter Granola Bar

This peanut bar tastes like something you'd get from the vending machine, minus the thigh-inflating effects.

RESISTANCE IS FUTILE!

Mother Teresa, Kate Moss . . . maybe they could limit themselves to 100 calories of these tempting treats. But we seriously doubt it!

AUNTIE ANNE'S ORIGINAL PRETZEL
About ¼ of a pretzel
Don't get tied up in knots about it.

BAGEL, PLAIN, 4.5"
⅓ of 1 bagel
And that's without any cream cheese.

BURGER KING DOUBLE WHOPPER WITH CHEESE
1⁄10 of 1 burger
There's almost an entire day's worth of fat in one sandwich.

HAAGEN-DAZS CHOCOLATE CHIP COOKIE DOUGH ICE CREAM
2½ tablespoons
You're going to need a smaller cone.

KFC HOT WINGS
1¼ wings
Even with the bone in, you don't get much.

KRISPY KREME POWDERED STRAWBERRY-FILLED DOUGHNUT
⅓ of a doughnut
Barely enough to dunk in your coffee.

PEANUT M&M'S
10 candies
They've never looked so small before, have they?

McDONALD'S FRENCH FRIES, LARGE ORDER
⅛ of a serving, or 1 ounce
And forget about ketchup.

PAPA JOHN'S PAN CRUST CHEESE PIZZA, 12"
About ¼ of 1 slice
Still fattening, any way you slice it.

SARA LEE ORIGINAL CREAM CHEESECAKE
½ of 1 serving
You can always share your slice with a friend.

PART THREE: FOOD RULES

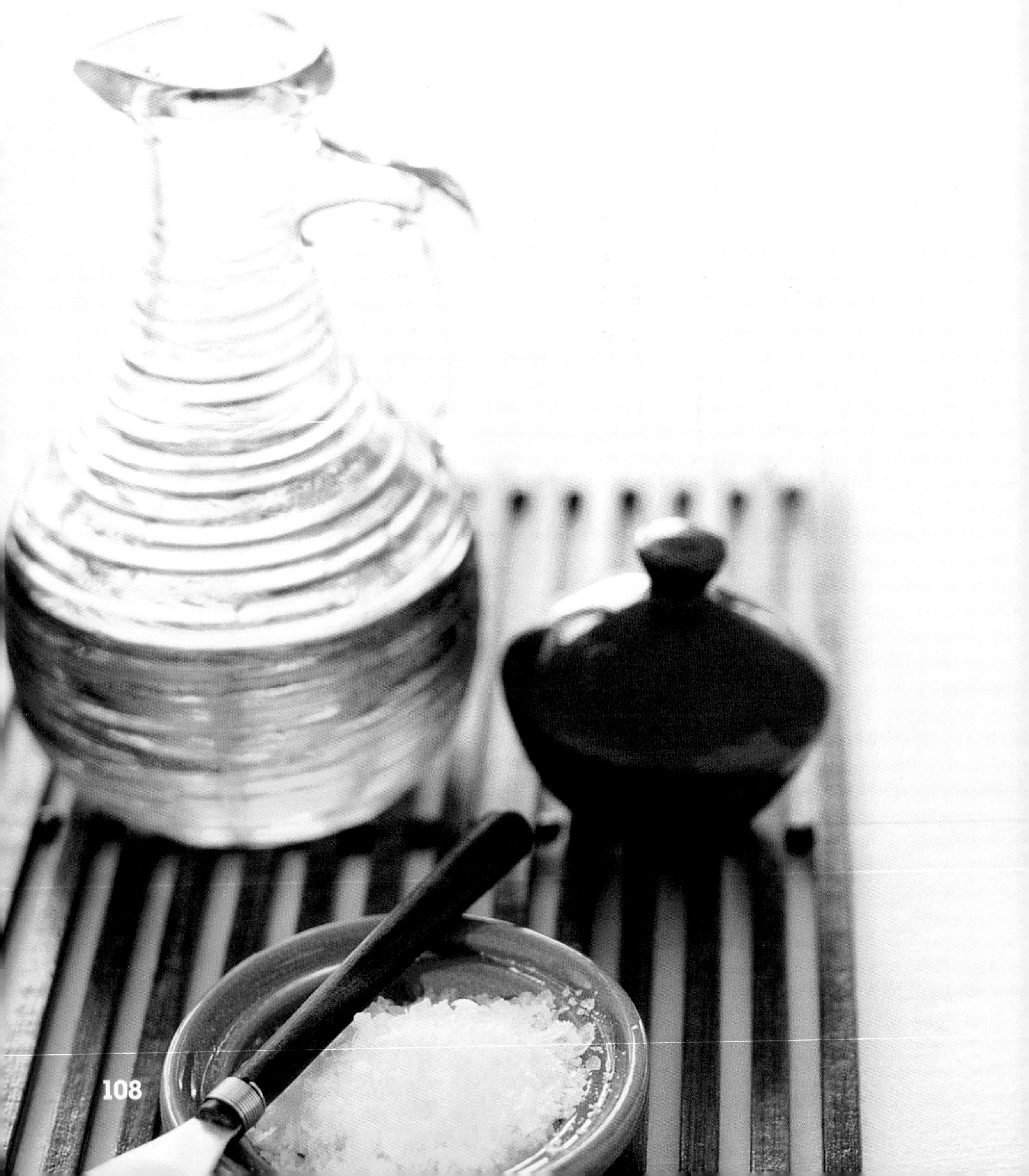

CHAPTER FIFTEEN

STEAL THESE MEALS

THESE FIVE FAST RECIPES FROM THE NATION'S TOP WEIGHT-LOSS CENTERS WILL MELT AWAY THE POUNDS—NOT YOUR WILLPOWER.

BY LENORA DANNELKE

WHEN THE STEAMY MONTHS ARRIVE, bare skin is in. To help you fill up without filling out, we asked five leading weight-loss centers for the best fat-fighting summer dishes. They're quick and delicious and top out at fewer than 400 calories per serving. You don't have to be the Naked Chef to throw them together, but add them to your meal rotation and you're bound to look and feel hotter in the buff.

Foods high in water and fiber allow you to eat mega-portions for mini calories. With 10 grams of fiber per cup—half the amount you should fill up on each day—garbanzo beans are weight-loss superstars.

Warm Garbanzo & Quinoa Salad

**C/O CHRISTIANA HEALTH CARE SYSTEM
IN WILMINGTON, DELAWARE**

Even if you usually have zero enthusiasm for veggie-only meals, give this one a shot. The mix of quinoa and beans is as hearty as a bowl of beef stew, and "olive oil, vinegar, and puréed scallions boost the flavor, so it doesn't have to be weighed down with fat," says nutrition manager Gabrielle Snyder Marlow, who cooks up meal plans for Christiana's 12-week personalized weight-loss plan, Fit4Life. The effect is pure comfort food in a bowl.

Butter doesn't have to be a no-no. Use a single pat on your potatoes at the table rather than adding it while you mash. Because you'll see it, you'll savor it more.

Chicken Marsala

**C/O HILTON HEAD HEALTH INSTITUTE,
HILTON HEAD ISLAND, SOUTH CAROLINA**

The secret to turning this Italian classic into a slim summer meal is using chicken cutlets, which are thinner than breasts, so your dose of lean protein cooks faster and more evenly without drying out. "Nobody likes dry chicken—but moist, tender chicken can feel like a treat," says Jen Welper, the chef at this posh beachside retreat for people serious about shedding pounds. Add mushrooms, shallots, and a splash of Marsala wine, and you're good to go.

Fresh herbs add flavor without the fat. Toss some chopped Italian parsley, basil, oregano, rosemary, and thyme into a dish and you'll forget you even have an oil cruet.

W|H

Fire-Roasted Wild Salmon with Stir-Fried Brown Rice

C/O MIRAVAL TUCSON, CATALINA, ARIZONA

Fiber is a cornerstone of the light-but-not-skimpy dishes at Miraval, a health resort where guests dine on local, in-season ingredients. Take this tempting stir-fry, made with unprocessed brown rice. Processing rice so it cooks faster removes the fiber along with the hull, says John D. Martin, Miraval's head kitchen honcho. His rule of thumb: Go for rice that needs to cook for 15 minutes or more per cup.

Missing red meat? You can sub beef for chicken; your clues to finding the leanest cuts are the words loin, ground, and center-cut.

Sizzling Fajitas

C/O THE ALBERT J. STUNKARD WEIGHT MAN-AGEMENT PROGRAM AT THE UNIVERSITY OF PENNSYLVANIA

Summer without Mexican food is like a piñata without candy. But south-of-the-border cuisine is usually filled with full-fat dairy, which piles on mucho flab. Luckily, there's always a way to reinvent fattening dishes, says Stunkard program director Andrea Diamond. She and her colleagues teach lifelong weight-loss skills, including how to trim the cals from Tex-Mex treats like these hot-to-handle fajitas by packing them full of veggies, low-fat dairy, lean protein, and spices.

Lemongrass has tough, fibrous outer leaves; peel them off and use only the lower two-thirds of the stalks. That's where you'll find the most flavor.

Lemongrass Ginger Whitefish

C/O PRITIKIN LONGEVITY CENTER & SPA, AVENTURA, FLORIDA

Hovering over a stove in the summer is as much fun as riding in an elevator full of sumo wrestlers. Which is why fish is a godsend. This low-fat belly shrinker tastes best barely seared, and pairs well with exotic flavors. "You can use small quantities of lemongrass and ginger but still get huge flavor," says Gayl Canfield, Ph.D., R.D., director of nutrition at Pritikin, where overnight spa guests take courses on topics from healthy grocery shopping to pumping iron.

Recipes

WARM GARBANZO & QUINOA SALAD

Prep: 20 min Cook: 5 min

1½ tsp chopped garlic

1 small zucchini, quartered and sliced

2 carrots, grated

½ c chopped red bell pepper

2 c canned garbanzo beans, rinsed and drained

½ c (packed) chopped scallions

2 Tbsp extra-virgin olive oil

3 Tbsp white-wine vinegar

¼ tsp salt

1 c quinoa or whole wheat couscous, cooked with vegetable broth according to package directions

4 c fresh baby spinach leaves, cleaned and dried

Coat a sauté pan with cooking spray and heat to medium-high. Add garlic, zucchini, carrots, and pepper. Sauté until softened, about 5 minutes, stirring frequently. Add beans and sauté until heated through.

In a food processor, purée scallions, gradually adding oil, vinegar, salt, and black pepper to taste. Process to a thick consistency.

Add scallion mixture and quinoa to sauté pan; heat through.

To serve, arrange 1 cup spinach on each of four plates and pile equal amounts of garbanzo bean mixture on top.

MAKES 4 SERVINGS.

PER SERVING: 292 cal, 10 g fat (1.4 g sat), 42 g carbs, 358 mg sodium, 10 g fiber, 10 g protein

W|H

CHICKEN MARSALA

Prep: 10 min Cook: 15 min

    3 Tbsp whole wheat flour
    3 Tbsp white flour
   ¼ tsp white pepper
1-1½ lb chicken cutlets
    3 c sliced mushrooms
    2 Tbsp thinly sliced shallots
   ½ c Marsala wine
   ½ c low-sodium chicken broth
    2 Tbsp chopped parsley
   ½ tsp chopped fresh thyme leaf

In a shallow bowl, combine flours and pepper. Dredge chicken in mixture and set aside.

Lightly coat a large, nonstick skillet with cooking spray and heat on medium-high. Add chicken and sauté until lightly browned, 2 to 3 minutes per side. Remove cutlets to a plate and keep warm.

Add mushrooms and shallots to pan; stir for 1 to 2 minutes.

Add wine to pan. Reduce to a glaze, scraping any loose brown bits from bottom of pan.

Reduce heat and add broth, parsley, and thyme. Stir; cook until broth reduces by half.

Return chicken to pan and simmer for 5 minutes. Serve hot.

MAKES 4 SERVINGS.

PER SERVING: 224 cal, 2 g fat (1 g sat), 20 g carbs, 400 g sodium,1 g fiber, 27 g protein

MAKE IT A MEAL Mash ½ cup boiled red bliss potatoes (leave the skins on for maximum nutrition) with 1 Tbsp fat-free cream cheese, 1 Tbsp skim milk, and salt and pepper to taste. Serve alongside ½ cup peeled, sliced carrots that have been boiled, drained, and glazed with 1 tsp honey. This pair of belly-filling sides adds a mere 116 calories, for a dinnertime total of 340.

FIRE-ROASTED WILD SALMON WITH STIR-FRIED BROWN RICE

Prep: 15 min   Cook: 30 min

- 2   tsp canola oil
- 1   16 to 20 oz wild salmon fillet, skinned
- 2   Tbsp chopped red bell pepper
- 2   Tbsp chopped celery
- 2   Tbsp thinly sliced scallions
- 2   tsp chopped cilantro
- 2   c cooked brown rice
- 4   c vegetable broth
- 4   bunches baby bok choy, sliced in half
- 1/2   c pineapple sauce

Pineapple sauce

- 1/2   tsp chopped shallots
- 1/2   red bell pepper, chopped
- 1/4   fresh pineapple, cored and chopped
- 1/2   tsp minced fresh ginger
- 2   Tbsp brown sugar
- 2   c pineapple juice
- 1   Tbsp rice-wine vinegar

Heat grill and preheat oven to 350°F. Brush 1 teaspoon oil on salmon and season with salt and pepper to taste. Grill for 3 to 4 minutes per side.

Transfer fish into an ovenproof dish and bake until flesh is just opaque, about 9 minutes. Set aside and keep warm.

To make stir-fried rice, heat a skillet over medium and add remaining oil. Add red pepper, celery, 1 tablespoon scallion, and cilantro to pan and sauté until crisp-tender. Add rice to pan and stir. Add vegetable broth and season with salt and pepper to taste. Let mixture cook until all vegetable stock is absorbed into rice, stirring occasionally. Remove from heat, cover, and set aside.

Fill a medium pot with water and bring to a boil. Meanwhile, place sauce ingredients in blender and process until smooth. (Makes about 2 cups.)

Blanch baby bok choy in boiling water until just tender but still bright green, 2 to 3 minutes.

To serve, place rice mixture in the bottom of a shallow serving bowl. Place salmon atop rice. Arrange baby bok choy around salmon and drizzle sauce around dish. Garnish with remaining scallion.

MAKES 4 SERVINGS.

PER SERVING: 352 cal, 10 g fat (1.5 g sat), 36 g carbs, 253 mg sodium, 5 g fiber, 27 g protein

SIZZLING FAJITAS

Prep: 10 min Cook: 15 min

2 tsp olive oil

½ red or white onion, sliced

1 red, orange, or green bell pepper, sliced

2 cloves garlic, minced

2 whole chicken breasts, grilled and cut into strips, or 8 oz extra-lean (95 percent lean) ground beef

½ c salsa

¼ c nonfat sour cream

4 whole wheat tortillas, 7"-8" in diameter (Variation: spinach or corn-flour tortillas)

1 c shredded low-fat mozzarella cheese

Heat olive oil in a medium skillet. Add onion, pepper, and garlic and sauté briefly. Add meat, reduce heat to medium, and sauté until no longer pink, about 10 minutes.

Stir in salsa and chili powder to taste. Sauté for 5 more minutes.

Spread 1 tablespoon sour cream in a thin layer on each tortilla. Divide the meat mixture on top of tortillas, sprinkle each with cheese, wrap, and serve.

MAKES 4 SERVINGS.

PER SERVING: (Chicken): 222 cal, 7 g fat (3.5 g sat), 27 g carbs, 504 mg sodium, 3 g fiber, 15 g protein. (Beef): 263 cal, 9.5 g fat (4 g sat), 27 g carbs, 526 mg sodium, 3 g fiber, 22 g protein

MAKE IT A MEAL Whisk together 2 Tbsp diced cilantro with 1 Tbsp light olive oil, 1 tsp lime juice, and garlic powder to taste. Toss 2 cups each hearts of palm, sliced tomatoes, and cucumber with dressing.

LEMONGRASS GINGER WHITEFISH

Prep: 15 min Cook: 5 min

- 1 Tbsp chopped lemongrass
- 1 tsp minced fresh ginger
- 2 cloves minced fresh garlic
- 2 Tbsp fresh lemon juice
- ½ jalapeño pepper
- 1 16 to 20-oz whitefish fillet

In a food processor, purée lemongrass, ginger, garlic, lemon juice, and jalapeño.

Rub mixture onto fish and marinate for 5 minutes.

Heat a heavy-bottomed pan on high. Place fillet in pan and sear for 2 minutes. Flip fish and reduce heat to medium. Cook for two more minutes. Divide onto four plates and serve hot.

MAKES 4 SERVINGS.

PER SERVING: 158 cal, 7 g fat (1 g sat), 2 g carbs, 58 mg sodium, <1 g fiber, 22 g protein

MAKE IT A MEAL Add 1 cup spinach steamed in 1 Tbsp white wine, 1 medium-size sweet potato (microwaved), and a salad made with 3 cups spring mix, chopped tomato, and chopped cucumber dressed with 1 Tbsp aged balsamic vinegar. Even with all those extras, this dinner still rings in under 350 calories.

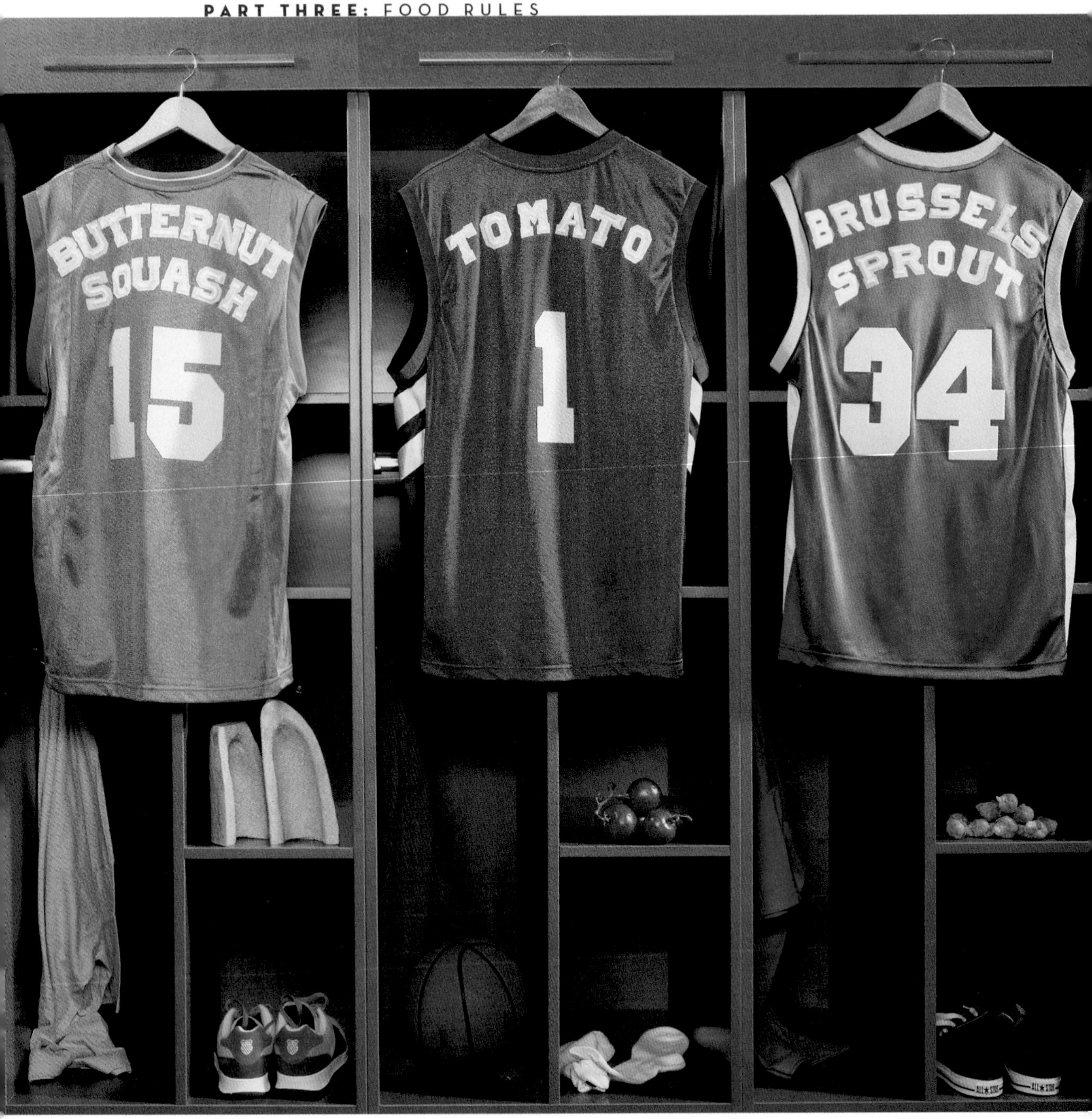
BUTTERNUT SQUASH
15
TOMATO
1
BRUSSELS SPROUT
34

CHAPTER SIXTEEN

VEGGIE MADNESS!!!

IN THE BIGGEST (ER, ONLY) TOURNAMENT OF ITS KIND IN THE HISTORY OF TUBERS, LEAFY GREENS, AND CRUCIFERS, WE PIT VEGGIE AGAINST VEGGIE IN A SCINTILLATING SMACKDOWN TO DECIDE ONCE AND FOR ALL THE MVP OF THE PRODUCE AISLE.

BY MATTHEW KADEY, R.D.

THIS MARCH, FORGET ABOUT UCLA taking on Duke in the NCAA finals. There's an even more important battle going on right here—between big-name contenders from broccoli to turnips. The goal: to determine which vegetable is No. 1 in nutrition. Of course, all veggies are winners when it comes to warding off excess weight and preventing disease; but with all the peeling and chopping you have to do to get them to the table, they're not the easiest foods around (no wonder most women fail to score five servings a day). So it's important to pick the stuff that packs the most vitamins and minerals. That's what this tourney is all about. After the champions emerge, turn to page 126 for the fastest, best-tasting ways to serve them up.

The Game Is On! Veggie vs. Veggie

To form our four starting divisions, we sorted vegetables by color (red, green, yellow/orange, and white). Then we chose the top 16 based on their levels of vitamin C, the water-soluble antioxidant whose list of health benefits is longer than Shaq's inseam. (To name just a few:cupboosts immunity, protects skin from sun damage, aids in healing wounds, and helps the body absorb iron.) Next, we pitted veggies against each other within their divisions to find out which ranked highest in the four nutrients women need most.

1. ROUND ONE FOLATE: You've heard of folic acid thanks to its success in making healthy babies.

RED DIVISION

GREEN DIVISION

ROUND ONE FOLATE

Red Bell Pepper vs. Red Cabbage
42 mcg vs. 13 mcg

Brussels Sprouts vs. Green Bell Pepper
54 mcg vs. 16 mcg

Tomato vs. Turnip
27 mcg vs. 20 mcg

Broccoli vs. Kale
55 mcg vs. 19 mcg

ROUND TWO MAGNESIUM

Red Bell Pepper vs. Tomato
11 mg vs. 20 mg

Brussels Sprouts vs. Broccoli
20 mg vs. 18 mg

In 1998 the U.S. government mandated that folic acid be added to grains, and by 2003 birth defects had dropped by a third. But the perks of getting the RDA (400 micrograms) of this mighty B vitamin don't stop there. Folate lowers CRP and homocysteine, two blood compounds that trigger artery inflammation, says Kathy McManus, R.D., director of the department of nutrition at Brigham and Women's Hospital in Boston. Studies find that a higher CRP rate raises sudden heart attack risk, and other data link high homocysteine levels with stroke and vascular disease. Another large-scale study found that women who got the most folate had the lowest incidence of breast cancer.

2. ROUND TWO MAGNESIUM: Because this mineral is found primarily in good-for-you foods like veggies (not Doritos), three out of four people in the U.S. don't get the 320 milligrams they need every day, says Elizabeth Somer, R.D., the author of *Age-Proof Your Body.* Which is a shame, since a study in the *Journal of the American College of Nutrition* found that low magnesium levels elevate blood

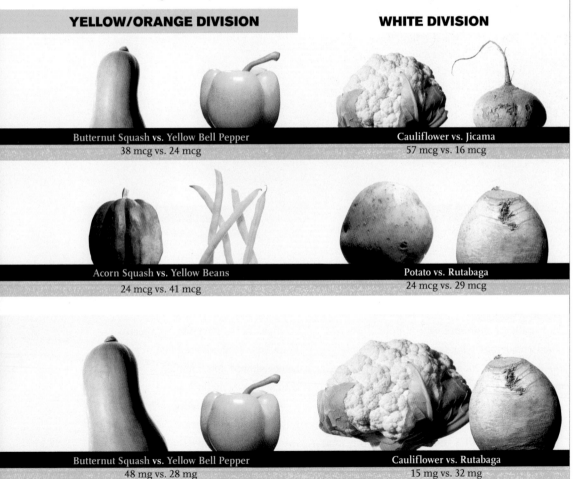

YELLOW/ORANGE DIVISION

Butternut Squash **vs.** Yellow Bell Pepper
38 mcg vs. 24 mcg

Acorn Squash **vs.** Yellow Beans
24 mcg vs. 41 mcg

Butternut Squash **vs.** Yellow Bell Pepper
48 mg vs. 28 mg

WHITE DIVISION

Cauliflower **vs.** Jicama
57 mcg vs. 16 mcg

Potato **vs.** Rutabaga
24 mcg vs. 29 mcg

Cauliflower **vs.** Rutabaga
15 mg vs. 32 mg

ROUND THREE IRON

Tomato **vs. Brussels Sprouts**
0.49 mg vs. 1.23 mg

ROUND FOUR SELENIUM

Brussels Sprouts **vs.**
1.4 mcg vs.

sugar levels. (When blood sugar hits a Rocky Mountain high, your pancreas pumps out more insulin, which makes your body store the sugar as fat, usually right around your middle. Then your blood sugar inevitably comes crashing down—along with your mood.) Magnesium also helps maintain normal muscle and nerve function, steadies heart rhythms, and supports your immune system.

3. ROUND THREE IRON: The monthly visit from Aunt Flo can leave you with an iron deficit when the mineral is lost through blood. And with-

out enough (the RDA is 18 milli-grams), your brain and muscles can't get enough oxygen, which slashes their efficiency. A recent Penn State study showed that iron defi-ciency slowed down female subjects completing mental tasks.

4. THE FINALS SELE-NIUM: This vital trace mineral mops up pesky free radicals and helps protect against heart dis-

Butternut Squash vs. Rutabaga
0.98 mg vs. 0.73 mg

Butternut Squash
0.7 mcg

WINNER!
Brussels Sprouts

ease, type 2 diabetes, and cancer. It also generates proteins your immune system needs to stay up and running. And your thyroid can't produce certain hormones without it. (While we blame hormones for a lot of bad stuff, they also happen to run our entire system—the thyroid hormones, for example, control the metabolism of every cell in your body.) Alas, women tend to come up short of the recommended 55 micrograms a day. The fix: Eat gobs of our final-four veggies, which are as rich in selenium, iron, magnesium, and folate as pro ballplayers are, well, rich.

TERRIFIC TWENTY

BY MAUREEN CALLAHAN, R.D.

DOUBLE-DRIZZLED SPROUTS

Preheat oven to 400°F. Cut 1 pound fresh brussels sprouts into halves and place on a foil-lined baking sheet. Drizzle with 1½ tablespoons olive oil and sprinkle with garlic salt and pepper. Roast for 14 to 18 minutes or until tender. Place sprouts in a bowl and drizzle with 1 teaspoon sherry vinegar or lemon juice.

MAKES 4 SERVINGS.

SLAM-DUNK SLAW

Finely shred ½ pound fresh brussels sprouts with the slicing blade of a food processor, mandoline, or knife. Whisk together 1 tablespoon extra-virgin olive oil, 2 teaspoons white wine vinegar, and ½ teaspoon Dijon mustard and drizzle over shredded sprouts. Toss gently and season with salt and freshly ground

black pepper. Divide into 2 bowls and sprinkle each with 1 tablespoon freshly grated Parmesan cheese and 1 teaspoon toasted chopped walnuts.

MAKES 2 SERVINGS.

"AWESOME, BABY!" LEMON SPROUTS

Bring a 16-ounce package of frozen petite brussels sprouts to a boil in ¼ cup water in a large sauce-pan. Cover and simmer for 10 minutes or until tender. Meanwhile, place 1 tablespoon butter in a medium microwave-safe dish, cover, and cook on high for 30 seconds or until butter is almost melted. Stir 1 teaspoon extra-virgin olive oil, ½ teaspoon finely grated lemon zest, and 1 teaspoon lemon juice into butter. Drain sprouts, toss with lemon-butter mixture, and season with coarse salt and freshly ground black pepper.

MAKES 4 SERVINGS.

OUT-OF-BOUNDS BRUSSELS SPROUTS WITH BACON

Finely shred ½ pound fresh brussels sprouts with the slicing blade of a food processor, mandoline, or knife. In a large nonstick skillet, cook 2 teaspoons olive oil and 1 strip bacon (chopped) over medium heat for 2 to 3 minutes or until bacon is crisp. Stir in ½ cup chopped onion and sauté for 4 minutes. Stir in shredded brussels sprouts and sauté for 6 to 8 minutes or until tender. Stir in 2 teaspoons chopped fresh thyme (or ¼ teaspoon dried) and season with coarse salt and freshly ground black pepper.

MAKES 2 SERVINGS.

CHERRY TOMATO THREE-POINT POPPERS

Preheat oven to 400°F. Rinse and drain 2 pints cherry tomatoes and place in a single layer on a baking sheet covered with foil. Drizzle with 2 teaspoons olive oil and season with salt and pepper. Roast 20 to 24 minutes, or until tomatoes collapse and begin to brown at the edges. Remove from oven and toss with a sprinkling of dill or your favorite herb. Use leftovers as toppers for pizza, crostini, sandwiches, or salad.

MAKES 4 SERVINGS.

FULL-COURT-PRESS BUTTERNUT CURRY

Steam 2 cups chopped butternut squash in the microwave on high for 6 to 8 minutes or boil it in a large saucepan for 10 to 12 minutes, until tender. Drain well. Heat 2 tablespoons olive oil in a large skillet. Stir in 1 teaspoon curry powder and cook for 1 minute. Stir in cooked squash and toss gently until well coated. Sauté for 1 to 2 minutes or until squash begins to brown. Stir in 1 tablespoon chopped fresh cilantro and season with salt and pepper.

MAKES 4 SERVINGS.

RUTABAGA WITH NOTHING-BUT-NET-MEG BUTTER

Peel 1 rutabaga and chop into half-inch chunks. Place in a microwave-safe dish with ½ cup water, cover with plastic wrap, and cook on high for 8 to 10 minutes or until tender. Drain and remove to a bowl. Add 2 teaspoons butter and a pinch nutmeg to a small skillet and cook over low heat until butter starts to brown. Remove from heat immediately and stir in rutabaga. Toss gently until vegetable is coated evenly with glaze.

MAKES 2 SERVINGS.

RUN-AND-GUN SQUASH SOUP

Thaw a 10-ounce package of frozen mashed butternut or winter squash in the fridge overnight or in the microwave on half power for 3 to 5 minutes. In a large saucepan, heat 1 tablespoon olive oil over

(continued)

TERRIFIC TWENTY—Continued

medium heat, then add 1 cup diced onions and sauté for 6 to 8 minutes or until tender. Stir in thawed squash, a 14-ounce can vegetable broth, and ½ cup apple cider. Bring to a boil; reduce heat and simmer for 5 minutes. Purée in a blender with lid slightly ajar so steam can escape. Season with salt and pepper. Ladle soup into two bowls and sprinkle with 1 tablespoon chopped chives or parsley.

MAKES 2 SERVINGS.

FAST-BREAK BROCCOLI WITH GARLIC CRUMBS

Heat 2 tablespoons olive oil in a large saucepan over medium heat. Stir in 2 to 3 cloves garlic (minced) and sauté for 1 minute. Stir in ½ cup whole wheat bread crumbs and continue cooking, stirring frequently, until bread crumbs brown lightly. Remove crumbs to a bowl; wipe out pan and fill with 2 inches of water. Bring to a boil over high heat and stir in 1 bunch broccoli, cut into bite-size pieces. Reduce heat to medium-low and let broccoli simmer for 5 to 7 minutes or until tender. Drain well and toss with bread crumb mixture. Season with salt and pepper and serve.

MAKES 6 SERVINGS.

PLAYMAKER RED PEPPER STIR-FRY

Cut 1 large seeded red bell pepper into thin 2-inch-long strips. Put ½ teaspoon peanut oil in a small nonstick skillet over medium-high heat. Add ¼ teaspoon minced garlic and stir-fry for 30 seconds.

Mix in bell pepper and stir-fry for 1 to 2 minutes, or until tender but still crunchy. Stir in 4 thinly sliced shiitake mushroom caps and cook for 2 minutes. Add ¼ cup thinly sliced scallion and cook for 1 minute. Remove from heat. Whisk 1 teaspoon rice vinegar, ½ teaspoon toasted sesame oil, and ⅛ teaspoon chili garlic sauce. Pour mixture over vegetables and toss gently to mix. Season with salt and serve.

MAKES 1 SERVING.

THE COMMISH'S CREAMED CAULIFLOWER

Bring 1 cup vegetable broth to a boil in a large saucepan. Stir in 5 cups fresh cauliflower florets (or thawed frozen florets) and return to boiling. Reduce heat, cover, and simmer for 7 to 9 minutes, or until cauliflower is tender. With a slotted spoon, transfer cauliflower into a serving dish and cover. Raise heat to high and bring broth to a boil for 4 to 5 minutes or until liquid is reduced to about 2 table-spoons. Whisk in ¼ cup light sour cream, 3 table-spoons chopped fresh chives, and 2 teaspoons coarse mustard (with seeds). Return cauliflower to pan and toss with sour cream mixture. Season with salt and pepper and serve.

MAKES 4 SERVINGS.

YELLOW BEANS WITH GOT-GAME GREMOLATA

Crush 1 tablespoon sliced almonds with your hands and toast in a skillet over medium heat for 2 to 3 minutes, turning frequently. Finely chop 1 table-spoon parsley and place in a large bowl with almonds, ½ teaspoon minced garlic, ¼ teaspoon finely grated lemon zest, 2 teaspoons lemon juice, and 2 teaspoons extra-virgin olive oil. Trim 1 pound yellow string beans. In a large saucepan, bring 2 inches' worth water to a boil. Add beans; cover and reduce heat to medium-low. Cook for 5 to 7 minutes or until tender. Toss beans with gremolata (the almond–lemon juice mixture) and season with a pinch of salt and pepper. Serve hot or cold.

MAKES 4 SERVINGS.

TAKE IT TO THE RIM TUSCAN KALE

Remove tough stems from 1 bunch kale and shred leaves. Heat 2 tablespoons olive oil in a large saucepan. Add 3 cloves garlic (minced) and sauté for 1 minute. Stir in ¼ teaspoon crushed red pepper flakes and ½ teaspoon oregano and cook for 1 minute. Option 1: Add shredded kale and ½

cup vegetable broth to pot, cover, and simmer for 10 to 15 minutes or until kale is tender. Option 2: Add shredded kale, 2 cups vegetable broth, and 1 14.5-ounce can Mexican stewed tomatoes (chopped) and simmer for 10 minutes. Season either version with salt and pepper.

MAKES 4 SERVINGS.

WIDE-OPEN GREEN PEPPER SALAD

Seed and chop 1 small green bell pepper and place in a small bowl. Stir in 2 tablespoons crumbled feta cheese, 1 tablespoon finely chopped red onion, and ½ tablespoon chopped fresh oregano (or ¼ teaspoon dried). Whisk together 1 teaspoon red wine vinegar and ¼ teaspoon Dijon mustard in a small bowl, then add 2 teaspoons extra-virgin olive oil. Drizzle over pepper mixture, toss gently, and season with salt and pepper.

MAKES 1 SERVING.

COAST-TO-COAST CIDER CABBAGE

Place 1 tablespoon olive oil in a large saucepan over medium heat. Stir in 1 cup chopped red cabbage and sauté for 4 minutes. Add ½ cup finely chopped apple and continue cooking for 2 to 3 minutes or until apple is tender. Then add ⅓ cup water, ¼ cup apple cider, and 2 tablespoons apple cider vinegar. Bring to a boil; cover and simmer for 10 minutes. Season with salt and pepper.

MAKES 4 SERVINGS.

(continued)

DUNKADELIC DIJON TURNIPS

In a small dish, blend 1 tablespoon butter, 1 teaspoon honey mustard, and 1 teaspoon olive oil with a fork. Cover and set aside. Peel 2 turnips and cut into half-inch pieces. In a large saucepan, bring turnip pieces to a boil in ½ cup water, then cover and simmer for 22 to 26 minutes or until tender. Drain well and place in a serving bowl. Stir in butter mixture and 3 tablespoons chopped fresh parsley; toss gently to combine. Season with salt and pepper.

MAKES 4 SERVINGS.

HOOP DREAMS HONEY SQUASH

Preheat oven to 400°F and brush a baking dish lightly with olive oil. Cut 2 small, unpeeled acorn squash crosswise into half-inch-thick rings. Scrape seeds out of the center of each ring and discard. Place rings in a large baking dish, spreading them out to keep them in a single layer with some overlap. Brush 1 tablespoon olive oil over rings and sprinkle with salt and pepper to taste. Bake for 20 minutes or until tender and beginning to brown lightly. Remove from oven. Drizzle 1 tablespoon honey over baked squash and sprinkle with 2 tablespoons finely chopped walnuts. Return pan to oven and bake for 6 to 8 minutes or until nuts are lightly browned.

MAKES 4 SERVINGS.

PICK 'N ROLL SHERRY PEPPERS

Preheat broiler. Cut 1 orange or yellow bell pepper in half lengthwise and remove seeds and veins. Place pepper halves, skin side up, on a foil-lined baking sheet. Flatten pepper with your hands. Broil for 7 to 9 minutes or until skin blackens. Remove from oven. Bring edges of foil together and seal to make a tightly closed package. Let pepper steam in package for 15 minutes. Remove skin and slice pepper lengthwise into thin strips and place in a bowl. Whisk together 1 teaspoon sherry and 1 teaspoon olive oil. Stir in 1 teaspoon chopped fresh thyme (or ⅛ teaspoon dried). Drizzle vinegar mixture over peppers and toss gently to mix. Season with salt and pepper.

MAKES 1 SERVING.

JUMP-BALL JICAMA SALAD

Peel 1 small jicama and cut in half lengthwise. Shave
each half into very thin slices using a mandoline or
sharp knife and place in a bowl. Peel 1 small red
beet and shave into very thin slices. In another bowl,
whisk together 2 tablespoons orange juice and 1½
teaspoons extra-virgin olive oil and pour over jicama-
beet mixture. Toss gently to mix; season with salt
and pepper.

MAKES 2 SERVINGS.

ALLEY-SCOOP
POTATO POCKETS

Prick 1 medium russet potato several times with a
fork and microwave on high for 8 to 10 minutes, until
tender. Let cool slightly; cut in half. Scoop out flesh,
leaving a quarter-inch border next to skin, into a
bowl. Add 3 tablespoons reduced-fat buttermilk, 1
thinly sliced scallion, 1 tablespoon finely chopped
sun-dried tomato pieces in olive oil, and 1 teaspoon
butter; mash with scooped-out potato. Season
potato mixture with salt and pepper and stuff back
into potato halves; sprinkle with 1 tablespoon
Parmesan cheese and broil until bubbly.

MAKES 1 SERVING.

■ **PART FOUR**

target practice

Get the results you want from your workouts! The following workouts focus on a specific fitness goal. Want a firmer, more shapely butt? Get it with Glute Camp on page 173. Looking for a flat, firm belly? We've got you covered with Is It Hot in Here? on page 161. Want smooth moves and increased agility? Turn to page 151. The results you want are at your fingertips!

CHAPTER SEVENTEEN

YOU REALLY SHOULD GET OUT MORE! (YEAH, YOU!)

IT'S NEVER TOO LATE TO SHAPE UP FOR SUMMER! WITH THESE 30-MINUTE OUTDOOR WORKOUTS, YOU CAN BUFF YOUR BODY—AND STILL HAVE TIME TO PLAY.

BY PAIGE GREENFIELD

TOTAL FITNESS GUIDE 2009

W|H

GIVEN A CERTAIN BABY-DADDY with an affinity for bongos and nekkedness, it's pretty clear that outdoor workouts are effective. But since gawking isn't exactly scientific evidence, we did some actual research. And guess what? The McConaughey Theory of Hotness is totally valid. Simply taking your running routine out of the gym ups calorie burn by about 5 percent, thanks to wind and varied terrain. And fluctuating outdoor temps further increase the number of calories you torch by about 7 percent because your body has to work to keep your thermostat dialed in to 98.6 degrees. Not convinced? Recently, researchers in England found that outdoor workouts are nature's Zoloft. When they compared the mental benefits of a 30-minute walk in the park with an indoor jaunt, 71 percent of the subjects who took it outside said they felt less tense afterward, while 72 percent of the indoor crew felt even more stressed.

A harder body and a brighter outlook? That's enough to make us ditch the fluorescents for the sun. So we asked fitness pros to craft some killer open-air workouts. The resulting 30-minute sweat sessions will get your blood pumping at any track, pool, park, or trail. Go on—get out there!

50:50

WORKS SHOULDERS, TRICEPS, CHEST, BACK, ABS, WAIST, HAMSTRINGS, AND INNER AND OUTER THIGHS

Standing in chest-deep water at the shallow end of the pool, extend your arms down along the sides of your body with your palms facing behind you. Keep your left leg straight and lift it back so your toes are 6 to 12 inches from the pool bottom. With your chest up, abs braced, and neck in line with your spine, inhale for five counts while quickly pumping your arms forward (A) and back (B), a few inches in each direction, without bending your elbows. Continue pumping as you exhale for 5 seconds. That's 1 rep. Do 5. Repeat on the other leg.

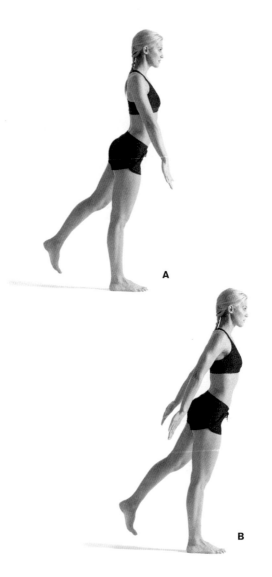

A

B

POOLATES SQUAT

WORKS ABS, BACK, GLUTES, AND QUADS

Stand with your feet hip-width apart on a kickboard (we like the Speedo Deluxe Training Board, $8, speedo.com) in the shallow end. Extend your arms out at shoulder height for balance (A). With your weight holding the kickboard toward the bottom of the pool, squat down until your thighs are almost parallel to the pool floor (B). Hold this position for 30 seconds, then try to stand up. Do 10 reps. Note: Allow plenty of space from walls or other people.

THE WORKOUT
POOLATES

WHY THE POOL? It lets you move in three dimensions instead of two, explains Rebecca Pfeiffer, M.P.H., a certified Pilates instructor and Poolates creator. "This gives your core and waist a deeper workout than you get on land," Pfeiffer says. While traditional aqua exercises use the water's buoyancy to make exercises easier, Poolates takes advantage of water's resistance for an extra challenge. "You engage all your major muscles to stay balanced, so each move works your entire body, not just the part you're targeting."

W|H

STEP STAR

WORKS ARMS, ABS, WAIST, BACK, GLUTES, HAMSTRINGS, QUADS, AND CALVES

Get into plank position with your feet together on the pool bottom and your hands on a pool step (water shouldn't come above your elbows) (A). Lift your right arm straight up as you rotate your hips and torso to the right until your body forms a T and you're balancing on your left arm (B). At the same time, raise your right leg to hip height (C). Return to the T position and then to start. Repeat on the opposite side. That's 1 rep. Do 4.

A

B

C

DOWNWARD LOG

STRETCHES AND STRENGTHENS ENTIRE BODY

Kneel facing a large log (a stable fallen branch or tree trunk) about 2 feet in front of you. Place your hands shoulder-width apart on the log, then straighten your legs so you're in a downward-dog position with your neck in line with your spine (A). Rise onto the balls of your feet (B). Lift your right leg and bend your right knee until your thigh is parallel to the ground and your heel points toward the sky (C). Hold for two counts. Lower your leg, coming down to flat (or as flat as possible) feet, and repeat on the other side. That's 1 rep. Do 10.

A

B

C

TOTAL FITNESS GUIDE 2009

W|H

TRAIL CORE STABILIZER

WORKS CORE STRENGTH AND AGILITY

Grab a lightweight branch (at least as long as your shoulders are wide) and hold it a bit lower than chest height with your elbows close to your torso (A). Brace your abs and start running as hard as possible, using the branch to prevent your arms and shoulders from swinging (B). Continue for 4 minutes.

A

B

SWING LUNGE

WORKS GLUTES, HAMSTRINGS, AND QUADS

Stand with your back about one giant step from a
1- to 2-foot-high swing. Reach back with your right
foot and place your toes on the seat (A). With your
arms at your sides, sink into a lunge until your
left thigh is parallel to the ground (B). Slowly return
to start. That's 1 rep. Do 10, then repeat on the
other side.

A

B

THE WORKOUT
STRENGTH

WHY THE PARK? It has great tools, like swings,
benches, and monkey bars. We asked exercise
physiologist Tom Holland, a personal trainer in
Darien, Connecticut, to put a new spin on some
of his favorite moves of all time—squats, lunges,
and chinups. Do the moves as a circuit—going
immediately from one move to the next. That's
one set. Rest for 2 minutes, then repeat for a
total of three sets. Nice work. You've earned a
trip to the Good Humor truck.

MONKEY-UPS

WORKS BICEPS, CORE, AND BACK

Jump up and grab a monkey bar with your hands
shoulder-width apart and palms facing you. Hang
from the bar with your arms straight, your knees
slightly bent, and your ankles crossed (A). Pull
yourself up until your chin passes the bar (B). Take
3 seconds to lower yourself. Do up to 10 reps.

BENCH JUMP

WORKS CORE, GLUTES, HAMSTRINGS, QUADS, AND HEART

Begin by standing on a 1 to 2-foot-high backless park bench with your knees slightly bent and your arms straight out in front of you at shoulder height (A). Jump down so you're straddling the bench (B). Jump back onto the bench, landing with your feet together. Continue jumping down and up as quickly as possible for 20 seconds.

A

B

SWING PIKE PUSHUP

WORKS SHOULDERS, BICEPS, CHEST, CORE,
AND BACK

Get in plank position with the tops of your feet on the
seat of a 1- to 2-foot-high swing (A). Press your arms
and feet down as you lift your hips toward the sky so
your body is in a pike position (B). Lower your hips to
the starting position, then immediately sink down into
a pushup (C). That's 1 rep. Do 10.

A

B

C

THE WORKOUT
ENDURANCE

WHY THE TRACK? "Muscular endurance is your muscles' ability to contract over a long period of time, and it increases through short bursts of high-intensity exercise and interval training," says Dori Madsen, a personal trainer in Park City, Utah. This also means that muscle-endurance training burns calories faster than Oprah doles out millions. The track provides easy, measurable distances that you can mark off for sprints, laps, and other interval exercises; and the bleachers or stadium stairs force you to use your own power (versus the treadmill's belt or the weight machine's cables). The less assistance you have when doing exercises, the more endurance you'll build.

WARMUP Jog around the track for 5 to 10 minutes at an easy pace.

BOOT CAMP INTERVAL BLAST Mark off 20 to 50 feet of a straightaway (start short if you haven't laced up your sneakers since October). Use the yard lines on the football field to estimate distance: 50 feet is about 17 yards.

1. Start at one mark and sprint as fast as you can to the next. Jog backwards to the start.

2. Run to the grass and do 25 to 50 crunches.

3. Repeat step one.

4. Run to the grass and do 10 to 20 pushups.

5. Return to the start and chassé (step with the left foot and hop your right foot forward to catch up with it) for 20 to 50 yards. Immediately grapevine back to the start. (Standing sideways, step with the left foot, cross the right one over it, step out with the left again, and step behind it with the right one.)

6. Walk one lap (a quarter mile) around the track.

7. Run up the stadium stairs, taking two at a time for 3 minutes, then carefully jog down.

8. Walk around the track for 3 minutes.

9. Repeat the entire circuit.

CHAPTER EIGHTEEN

FAST AND FEARLESS

OUR 20-MINUTE WORKOUT SERIES WILL MAKE YOU THE MOST GRACEFUL BADASS IN TOWN.

BY JENNY EVERETT

WANT TO KNOW THE DEFINITION of agility? Check out those adorable pooches that tear up the obstacle courses on ESPN2. They can run at top speed, stop short, change direction, and start again, all in a fraction of a second. You need similar skills so your muscles can react Jack Russell–fast, whether you're blowing by an opponent or dodging people at a crowded airport.

We asked our fitness columnist, Amy Dixon, an exercise physiologist and the group fitness manager at Equinox in Santa Monica, California, to design a workout that will fine-tune your agility. Do the moves 2 nonconsecutive days a week and we guarantee you'll be fleet of foot in 4 weeks.

Fancy Footwork

Can't make it to the gym? Kill time during commercials with these three living-room-friendly agility drills from Mike Mejia, a certified strength and conditioning specialist and personal trainer on Long Island, New York.

Shuffle

Stand on the left side of an 8- to 10-foot-wide room (or rug) with your feet shoulder-width apart and hands at your sides. Step to your right, first with your right foot, then with your left, repeating all the way across the room as explosively as you can. When you get within a foot of the right wall, lean to the left to shift your momentum and shuffle back. Repeat five times.

Squat Thrusts

Stand with your feet together. Squat and place your palms on the floor outside your feet. With your arms mostly straight, jump your feet back into plank position. Then immediately jump your feet up between your hands and stand up. Repeat eight to 10 times.

Ladder Drill

Tape a 2-foot square on the floor. Straddle the box. Step quickly into the box with your right foot, followed by your left; then out with your right, and out with your left. Repeat 10 times. Switch the leading foot and do 10 more.

Video

Bonus intel! Go to womenshealthmag.com/20minuteworkout to view instruction videos of each move.

Agility Ability

Fine-tune your coordination in 4 weeks flat. Do these moves twice a week to train your muscles to respond quickly. Opt for a weight at which you can barely eke out the last rep of your final set with perfect form.

FOOTBALL FEET

WORKS GLUTES, HAMSTRINGS, QUADS,
AND CALVES

With your knees slightly bent, straddle a 12-inch-high
step or bench. Bend your elbows 90 degrees, palms
facing each other, and keep your hands in relaxed
fists (A). Allowing your arms to swing freely, step onto
the bench with your left foot, then with your right (B),
then step down with your right foot, followed by your
left (C). Continue as quickly as possible for 1 minute.
That's one set. Do three sets, resting for 30 seconds
between sets.

A

B

C

DUMBBELL SQUAT PRESS

WORKS SHOULDERS, GLUTES, HAMSTRINGS, QUADS, AND CALVES

Standing with your feet hip-width apart, place an 8- to 10-pound dumbbell outside each foot. With arms at your sides, squat until your thighs are parallel to the floor (A). Grab each dumbbell and straighten your legs while pressing the dumbbells overhead (B). Squat again and place the dumbbells on the floor. Return to standing. That's 1 rep. Do three sets of 10 to 12 reps, resting for 30 seconds between sets.

Trainer Tip

Place your weight on your heels and squeeze your glutes as you stand.

B

A

LATERAL HOP AND TOSS

WORKS UPPER BACK, SHOULDERS, TRICEPS,
HIPS, GLUTES, HAMSTRINGS, QUADS,
AND CALVES

Balance a 5- to 8-pound medicine ball on your left
palm and stand with your feet together and your
knees slightly bent. Lift your right foot about an inch
behind you (A). Hop to your right about 4 feet, tossing
the ball across your body and catching it in your right
hand as you land on your right foot (B). Repeat the
move to the left as quickly as possible. That's 1 rep.
Do three sets of 12 to 15 reps, resting for no more
than 30 seconds between sets.

A

B

SQUAT BOUNCE AND CATCH

WORKS SHOULDERS, BICEPS, TRICEPS, GLUTES, HAMSTRINGS, AND CALVES

Grab a 5- to 8-pound medicine ball with both hands and position your feet wider than shoulder-width apart. Hold the ball an inch in front of your chest and lower your hips until your thighs are parallel to the floor (A). Bounce the ball off the floor (B); as you catch it, jump as high as you can and push the ball straight overhead (C). That's 1 rep. Do three sets of 12 to 15 reps, moving as quickly as possible and resting for no more than 30 seconds between sets.

Trainer Tip

To really work your triceps, throw the ball down with serious force.

C

A

B

SWITCH LUNGE

WORKS CORE, GLUTES, HAMSTRINGS, QUADS, AND CALVES

Lunge forward with your right thigh parallel to the floor (A). Swinging your arms for balance and momentum, jump up and switch legs (B), landing in a lunge with your left foot forward (C). Repeat. That's 1 rep. Do three sets of 12 to 15 reps, resting for no more than 30 seconds between sets.

A

B

C

W|H

NUTCRACKER CURL

WORKS BICEPS, HIPS, GLUTES, HAMSTRINGS, QUADS, AND CALVES

Grab a 5- to 8-pound medicine ball with both hands and stand with your legs wider than shoulder-width apart, toes turned out. Let the ball hang straight down in front of you. Lower your hips until your thighs are parallel to the floor (A). Explode back up, using your momentum to propel you off the floor, and curl the medicine ball up to your chest (B). Land back in the squat position with arms straight down. That's 1 rep. Return to standing. Do two sets of 12 to 15 reps, moving quickly and resting for no more than 30 seconds between sets.

Trainer Tip

Focus on landing softly, and brace your core to help maintain your balance.

B

A

ROLLING PUSHUP

WORKS SHOULDERS, BICEPS, TRICEPS, CHEST,
CORE, BACK, AND HIPS

Get in plank position with your left hand on top of a
5- to 8-pound medicine ball and your right hand on the
floor. Lower into a pushup until your chest is as close
to the floor as possible (A). Press back up to plank.
Placing your weight on your right hand, roll the ball
across to the right (B), and then place your left hand
on the floor and your right hand on top of the ball. Do
another pushup, then roll the ball back to the left (C).
That's 1 rep. Do two sets of 6 to 10 reps, moving
quickly and resting for 30 seconds between sets.

A

B

C

CHAPTER NINETEEN

IS IT HOT IN HERE? OR IS IT ME?

EIGHT SERIOUS AB MOVES (AND ONE THAT'S REALLY INSANE) FROM TOP OLYMPIC TRAINERS THAT WILL SCORE YOU A ROCK-SOLID AND READY-TO-BARE MIDDLE IN JUST 4 WEEKS.

BY TED SPIKER

OLYMPIC ATHLETES POSSESS astounding physical prowess, whether they use it to smash records on the track, deftly wield a fencer's foil, or power a fastball to center field. You don't need us to tell you that. But make no mistake: All of these high performers get their skill and power from the same place: a bulletproof core.

And so do you—even if you're not cavorting around the Olympic Village in a red, white, and blue tracksuit. "The core is the mainframe of the body," says Peter Melanson, a strength and conditioning coach at the U.S. Olympic Training Center in Colorado Springs. It supplies power and is crucial for anything that requires strength or balance—from winning a chicken fight in the pool to lugging trash cans to the curb. And whatever you're doing, a strong midsection protects you from landing on the disabled list. "Power is the most important factor in performance," says Jonathan Carlock, a strength and conditioning coach with the U.S. Olympic Committee who works with sprint cyclists and track athletes.

For the select few, Amanda Beard–level core strength can mean the difference between Olympic gold and Olympic obscurity. But anyone can reap the rewards of a mean middle—you just need to know how to work it. Melanson says the biggest mistake people make is thinking that the more crunches they do, the faster they'll see a six-pack. The surprising truth, he says, is that you get better results by doing fewer reps with greater resistance.

That doesn't mean it's easy—hard abs take hard work, no matter what. We asked Melanson, Carlock, and Bo Sandoval, an Olympic strength and conditioning coordinator, to reveal the moves they use to torture the Olympians they coach. So get ready to chisel your middle in time for the opening ceremonies of the 2012 Olympics.

Do It

Train your core with these eight moves 3 nonconsecutive days a week. Either do them all together as a stand-alone workout or add three or four of them to the end of your usual strength-training routine. For each move, start with one set. Once you can complete all the reps with perfect form, add another.

HIP BRIDGE AND HEEL DRAG

WORKS CORE, GLUTES, HAMSTRINGS, QUADS, AND CALVES

Lie on your back with your lower legs on a stability ball. Raise your hips until they're aligned with your feet and shoulders (A). Raise your left leg until the bottom of your foot is facing the ceiling (B). Press your right heel into the ball and roll it toward your butt (C). Roll the ball back out. Keeping your hips lifted, repeat the rolling motion for 12 to 15 reps. Repeat on the other side, resting for 30 seconds beforehand if needed. That's one set. Do three sets, resting for 30 seconds between sets.

A

B

C

weight loss

Weight loss is about frying fat with metabolism-boosting workouts, eating foods that support your goals, understanding where hunger comes from and adjusting your eating habits accordingly, and finding strategies that work for you. All that and more is covered here. What are you waiting for? Start shedding the pounds with this valuable advice!

CHAPTER TWENTY-ONE

THE ABC'S OF SLIM

READY TO DITCH SOME POUNDS?
START WITH THE RIGHT VOCABULARY.

BY AMY PATUREL

A is for Alcohol

You booze, you lose: A daily serving of hooch may be better for keeping off weight than abstaining. Alcohol may increase leptin, a hormone that curbs your appetite for sweets. To get the perks with minimal calories, order a glass of sauvignon blanc (119 calories per 5 ounces).

B

is for Buddies

Researchers at the University of Pittsburgh School of Medicine compared solo dieters to teams of dieters. After 10 months, the latter were likelier to have maintained their loss (66 percent versus 24 percent). Find a bud 24/7 at weightlossbuddy.com.

is for Cortisol

Your adrenal glands secrete this stress hormone to help you handle threats, but too much can be bad news. Last year, researchers at the University of Leeds in the UK linked high levels of cortisol to increased snacking on junk food. Spend the cash you'd pay for a big dinner on a stress-reducing massage.

is for Density

A yearlong study published in the *American Journal of Clinical Nutrition* found women eating water-rich foods low in calories but high in nutrients (like veggies) as part of a low-fat diet lost more weight than those who only cut back on fat. They were less hungry than the low-fat-only bunch, too, most likely because they ate 25 percent more food by weight. Go for grub with an energy density (calories per serving ÷ weight in grams of serving) of 2 or less. Or snag ideas from Barbara Rolls's *The Volumetrics Eating Plan*, which lists the energy densities of dozens of foods.

is for Estimation

Developing an eye for appropriate serving sizes can make or break your diet. Commit these serving-size visuals to memory:

- 3 ounces lean meat = a standard deck of 52 cards
- $1/2$ cup of fruit, vegetables, or grains = half a baseball
- 1.5 ounces cheese = 3 dominoes

 **is for Fructose**

A study published last year in the journal *Hepatology* found that feeding fructose-laced water to rats increased their risk of obesity. Ditch the artificially sweetened juices and sodas and get your fructose from fruit—a form that researchers say could be kinder to your waistline.

 **is for Grapefruit**

Kick off every meal with half a ruby red or 8 ounces of grapefruit juice—you could speed up your weight loss. Subjects of a 2006 study in the *Journal of Medicinal Food* who ate half a grapefruit before each meal lost more weight after 12 weeks than those who didn't (3.5 pounds versus less than a pound).

 **is for Hydration**

Studies have shown that drinking water can slightly increase your caloric burn rate. The researchers behind one such study at Franz-Volhard Clinical Research Center in Berlin estimate that sipping six extra 8-ounce glasses a day can burn 17,400 more calories (about 5 pounds of fat) per year.

 **is for Insulin**

The amount of this sugar-regulating hormone you secrete may dictate the diet you should follow. A study published in the *Journal of the American Medical Association* found that high insulin secretors dropped about 13 pounds on a low-carb diet but only about 3 on a low-fat/higher-carb diet. Look in the mirror: If you store fat in your belly (have an "apple" body shape), you're more likely to secrete excess insulin and benefit from fewer carbs.

 **is for Journal**

If you write down everything you eat, research has shown, you can cut your intake by 500 to 1,000 calories a day. And you'll keep the weight off: Food journaling is one of the successful behaviors used by people in the National Weight Control Registry, a list of dieters who have maintained a loss of 30 pounds or more for at least one year.

is for Ketosis

The point at which your body runs low on carbs and starts burning fat stores for fuel, ketosis can jump-start a diet or bust a plateau. Studies show that dieters who restrict carbs typically lose more weight during the first 3 to 6 months, but after about a year their results are comparable to those who go low-fat. So after dropping those initial pounds, it's OK to have whole grain pasta and bread again—in moderation.

is for Leptin

Fat cells secrete this hormone to tell your brain you're full. But researchers have found that fasts and extremely calorie-restrictive diets can lower leptin levels, prompting you to eat more. To keep this hormone in balance, strive for a slow, steady weight loss—no more than 1 to 2 pounds per week.

m is for Milk

You might get better results from your workout if you imbibe moo juice. A study in the *American Journal of Clinical Nutrition* found that downing 2 cups of skim milk after intense weight-lifting workouts built more muscle and burned twice as much fat as drinking carbohydrate beverages (such as a sports drink). But go with real cow's milk—in the study, drinks made from soy had no effect.

is for Numbers

Nobody enjoys weigh-ins, but research shows that people who hop on the scale once a day are more likely to lose and to maintain their loss. Make a standing appointment for yourself—just don't obsess over the number you see.

is for Omelet

Eggs are an ideal protein source, says Jonny Bowden, Ph.D., C.N.S., author of *The 150 Healthiest Foods on Earth*. Protein helps build muscle, which will fry more calories per pound than fat. Bonus: You'll burn about 25 percent of the eggs' calories just by digesting them (protein metabolism uses more energy than that of fat and carbs). A two-egg omelet takes you a quarter of the way to your protein RDA.

is for Peanuts

Subjects in a study at Purdue University received about 500 calories' worth of peanuts a day to eat at their discretion. After 8 weeks, they had gained an average of about 2 pounds—much less than the 8 pounds researchers had predicted. Probable cause:

The high-protein and high-fiber nuts filled them up. And after 19 weeks, they also had boosted their resting metabolic rates by 11 percent, possibly due to the fatty acids in the nuts. Take the edge off your appetite by snacking on a handful (a quarter cup) per day.

 is for Quinoa

Quinoa (keen-wa) has more hunger-taming protein and fiber and less carbs than most other whole grains. Swap it for white rice and other refined grains.

is for Replacements

Researchers at the University of Kansas found that dieters who drank liquid meal replacements lost just as much weight over 52 weeks as those who used the weight-loss drug Orlistat with regular meals. Who needs pills?

TOTAL FITNESS GUIDE 2009

W|H

S
is for Stress

Scientists at Georgetown University fed two groups of mice a diet of high-fat, high-sugar feed and measured how much weight they gained. Stressed mice (you don't want to know how they pushed them over the edge) gained more than twice as much weight as the group with the same diet but no stress. The reason? Researchers believe that stress causes the release of a molecule that helps increase the size and number of fat cells. The next time you're feeling the strain, do yoga (see Y) instead of dessert.

is for Tea

The fat-busting benefits of green tea boil down to disease-fighting compounds called catechins. One study of 240 Japanese men and women found that when subjects drank green tea containing 583 milligrams of catechins per 12-ounce cup, they dropped more weight—and inches—than those who ingested tea containing only 96 milligrams. Max your results by steeping your bag of green tea as long as possible. The darker the hue of your brew (and the more bitter it is), the more catechin-rich the cup.

is for User-Friendly

A recent study in the *Journal of the American Medical Association* assigned 160 overweight and obese volunteers to one of four popular diets for 6 months. They found that the strongest predictor of weight loss wasn't the type of diet but compliance with the selected plan. The takeaway: Find a plan you can live with so you'll stick to it (e.g., if you need help controlling portions, try Weight Watchers' Core Plan).

is for Vinegar

A study published in the *Journal of the American Dietetic Association* found that swallowing 60 grams (about 4 tablespoons) of an apple cider vinegar mixture with a high-glycemic-index meal caused test subjects to eat 200 to 275 fewer calories over the rest of the day. If you can't stomach the stuff straight, try mixing it into a low-fat dressing.

is for Weights

If you've put off pumping iron, get to it. According to experts, you burn calories faster after a strength-training session than you would after a cardio session. And researchers at the University of Alabama at Birmingham found that lifting weights three times a week for 25 weeks caused women to lose an average of 4 pounds of body fat.

is for Xenical

This prescription fat blocker made news last year when the FDA greenlighted its over-the-counter version, Alli. But both drugs come with an unfortunate side effect: loose stools. We say pass on the gas and slim down the old-fashioned way.

is for Yoga

A study at the Fred Hutchinson Cancer Research Center in Seattle found that normal-weight women who practiced yoga for 4 or more years gained 3 pounds less over 10 years than those who didn't. Grab a mat and get going.

is for Z's

When you skimp on sleep, your brain thinks you're low on fuel and sends a message to your stomach to start growling. A study published in the *American Journal of Epidemiology* found that among 68,183 women, those who slept for 5 hours or less were an average of 5 pounds heavier than women who snoozed for 7 hours. Want to stay slim? Go to bed.

CHAPTER TWENTY-TWO

LOSE
WEIGHT
WITHOUT THE
MATH!

SICK OF DIETS THAT ARE MORE COMPLICATED THAN YOUR TAX RETURN? HERE'S HOW TO DITCH UNWANTED POUNDS–NO CALCULATOR REQUIRED.

BY PAIGE GREENFIELD

WITH ALL THE WEIGHING, measuring, and calorie totaling, dropping a few pounds can seem as mind-bending as high school calculus. But it doesn't have to be. "Of course calories count," says Dawn Jackson Blatner, R.D., a spokesperson for the American Dietetic Association, "but there are plenty of ways to cut them without a math Ph.D." In fact, some simple lifestyle changes are often more effective than obsessive number crunching. Follow these four strategies and the only figure you'll be thinking about is the smokin' one in the mirror.

INSTEAD OF THIS Counting calories

TRY THIS Joining a club

BECAUSE Keeping a running total is a little like guessing how many jelly beans are in a Mason jar. According to a 2006 study published in the *Annals of Internal Medicine*, Americans—even those who are at a healthy weight—consistently lowball the number of calories in large fast-food meals by up to 38 percent.

For portion control without the decimal points, sign up for a delivery service like DeliciouslyYours (ediets.com) or Health Management Resources (hmrprogram.com). They deliver meals in just-right sizes to your doorstep each week. And the foods they consist of are usually high in fiber and protein, so you won't feel deprived, says Anne Fletcher, R.D., author of *Thin for Life*.

Another, er, plus: The smaller portions train you to recognize proper serving sizes, so you'll make smarter choices when the prepackaged grub is out of reach. You can enroll in a meal-delivery service for $12 to $20 a day; there are good options in the freezer aisle too, says Elisa Zied, R.D., author of *So What Can I Eat?!* Look for frozen meals that have less than 500 calories and have at least 4 grams of fiber, no more than 15 grams of fat (fewer than 3 grams saturated and no trans fat), and fewer than 700 milligrams of sodium.

INSTEAD OF THIS Eating by food ratios

TRY THIS Eyeballing labels

BECAUSE If diets like the Zone, Atkins, or South Beach didn't work for you, it may not be because you couldn't give up bagels. It could be because you're too damn busy to bother updating percentages and ratios at every meal. If you don't have Rain Man keeping tabs on your meals, Try this instead:

Take 15 seconds to scan food labels for key ingredients. According to a 2007 report by the USDA Economic Research Service, we spend an average of 30 percent of our annual grocery bill on foods such as muffins, cakes, cupcakes, cookies, crackers, ice cream, candy, soda, and doughnuts—foods whose ingredients lists have sugar at or near the top. It's a pretty big duh that sweeteners jack up calories, but they also take your blood sugar on a roller-coaster ride that lands you right back at the fridge. We call it the theory of "calories in, calories in."

End the snacking madness by making natural, whole foods the bulk of your diet. That includes fruits, veggies, and lean meats such as chicken, turkey, flank steak, pork chops, and fish. And when stocking up on packaged foods, choose ones "that list whole foods, such as whole wheat flour, oats, peanuts, and real fruit, in the first line of ingredients," Zied says. That's your clue that a food is lower in calories and higher in fiber and protein than one with a lot of high-fructose corn syrup, sugar, molasses, or even honey.

INSTEAD OF THIS Logging 3 0 minutes on the treadmill

TRY THIS Pumping up to scale down

BECAUSE According to a recent review by a Duke University medical researcher, treadmill displays inflate the number of calories you burn by 10 to 15 percent. The study also found that 20 percent of us reward ourselves after exercise by eating as many calories as we worked off—and that we're less inclined to get physical after a strenuous workout for 2 to 6 hours. That's when we'll veg out on the couch instead of do housework.

A more efficient way to counteract dessert is to pump iron. Though cardio torches more calories minute-for-minute than lifting, weight training keeps your internal furnace going long after you put down the dumbbells. A study in the journal *Medicine & Science in Sports & Exercise* found that after 6 months of lifting weights three days a week, subjects increased their resting metabolic rate (that's the number of calories you burn just sitting on your butt) by 7 percent. To squeeze the most out of every curl and squat, speed it up: Another study in the same journal found that lifting quickly (for example, during a squat, lowering for 2 seconds, then coming up as fast as you can) fries calories 11 percent faster than lifting slowly. Researchers think the explosive movements create more calorie-melting muscle contractions.

INSTEAD OF THIS Measuring each bite
TRY THIS Enjoying each bite
BECAUSE Being a slave to your kitchen scale won't make the one in your bathroom budge faster. A 2007 study in the *American Journal of Clinical Nutrition* confirmed that it is possible to eat more and still slim down. The study compared weight loss in two groups of obese women. All of them were told to eat a reduced-fat diet, but one group was also instructed to consume a lot of water-rich foods, like soups, fruits, and vegetables. That group ate

25 percent more food by volume but lost more weight (an average of 17.5 pounds versus 14). How? They were eating fewer calories, but were still satisfied, thanks to the foods' high water content. "Physical activity was the same in both groups, so if the people in one group lost more, they had to have eaten fewer calories," says lead study author Barbara Rolls, Ph.D.

Instead of measuring your meals, try a more measured approach to eating. It takes your brain 12 to 15 minutes to receive the signal that your stomach is at max capacity, so wait for it. If you pause between bites, chances are you'll get that signal before you've scarfed down seconds. Don't have that kind of self-control? Choose foods that are impossible to bolt down: produce you have to peel, nuts in the shell, and spicy foods.

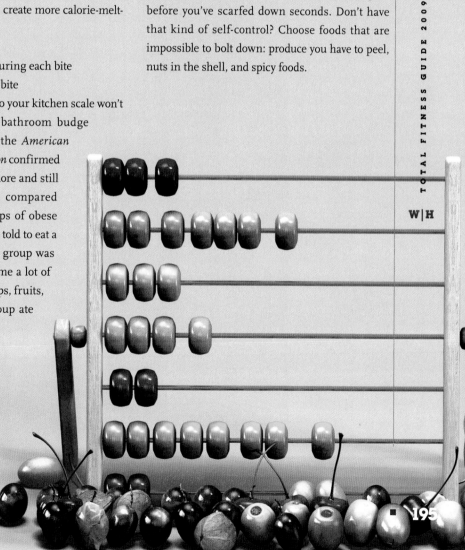

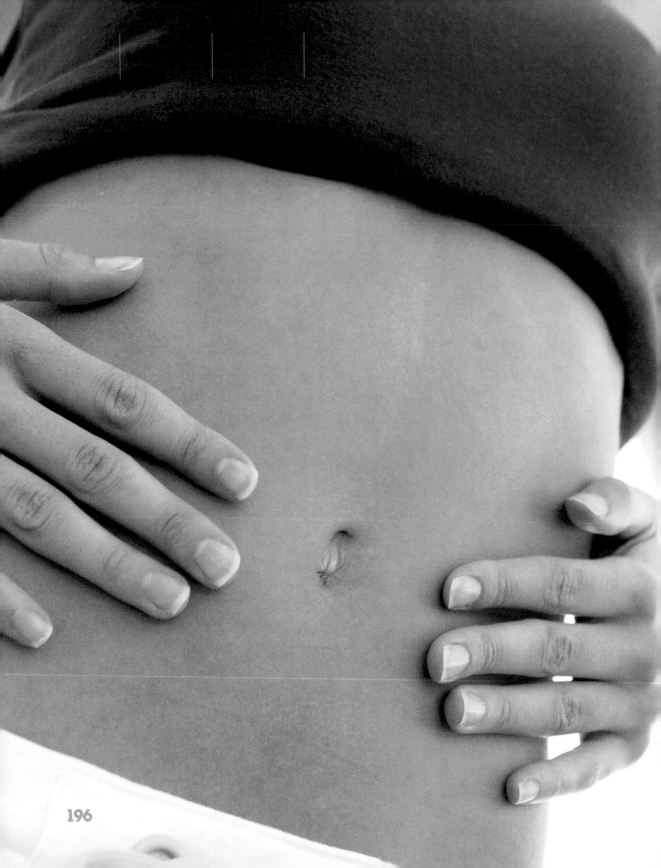

CHAPTER TWENTY-THREE

LISTEN TO YOUR GUT

THE REAL STORY BEHIND HUNGER PANGS– STRAIGHT FROM THE SOURCE

BY YOUR STOMACH, REPORTING BY MORGAN LORD

HEY, YOU. UP THERE. CAN WE TALK? I know you don't expect to hear from me except around mealtimes or after you've had Mexican food, but there's a lot about me you don't know. You think I'm a trouble-maker who sabotages your diet and makes you look bad in a two-piece. You think I'm an ingrate who's always complaining: too full, too empty, too spicy, too many beans.

OK, I see your point. And maybe all the growling doesn't help my image. But hear me out: I do more for you than you know. I work non-stop, 24 hours a day, with no breaks, and I usually pull a double on

Um... got a match?

That's fat padding your abdomen, not me spreading out.

Believe it or not, my size actually has nothing to do with yours: Bellies' dimensions are predetermined by genetics, and we don't grow in proportion to our owners. That's why some very svelte people can gulp down a lot of food without getting a gut. For instance, 98-pound Sonya Thomas, a competitive eater most famous for downing 39 hot dogs in 12 minutes, regularly defeats men four to five times her size. I sure don't envy her stomach.

So here's what I'm doing while you're tucking into a plate of ribs: The upper section of my bean-shaped body, or fundus, serves as a pantry, storing food until it travels through my central region, the corpus, to be processed by my lower half, or antrum. That's where all the actual work of digestion takes place. And it is work. I have to flex my muscles (yes, I do have them! They form the muscularis, the third layer of about five I have) in a rhythmic, agitating motion, like a washing machine, to mix your food with acid and digestive juices that break it down into its basic components: proteins, sugars, and fats.

It's a big job, but I have help from the 35 million acid-secreting glands in my lining. On a normal day, I produce 2 to 3 liters of gastric juices. Dropping all that acid (hey, a little stomach humor!) doesn't just help with digestion; it also kills bacteria, protecting you from infection. Normally, a healthy layer of mucus over my lining keeps me safe from the acid's harmful effects, but from time to time, you aggravate that layer—with a bacterial infection, or by popping aspirin like it's Pez—and acid can erode through. Too much of that kind of damage could mean—gulp—an ulcer. Every stomach's worst nightmare.

holidays. I kill the bacteria lurking in your food to protect you from disease. And most important, I help convert the food you eat into fuel for everything you do, from washing the dishes to running a marathon. So give me a little credit, why don't you, and cut out the pinching already. That's never going to make me any flatter.

Besides, those rolls you like to grab and call your "Buddha belly" aren't me. I'm high up in the abdomen, under the bottom of your rib cage, a little to the left. I'm also not as big as you think—only about 12 inches long and 4 to 10 inches wide when I'm empty. I can stretch to hold up to 3 liters of food—pretty impressive, right? That's why you need to unbutton your pants after stuffing yourself silly (ahem, need I remind you of the Super Bowl?). But don't go blaming me for your muffin top.

Anyway, after I've churned the food into a nice, mushy mixture called chyme, I squeeze it every 20 seconds through the pyloric sphincter, a strong ring of smooth muscle at the end of my food-passing canal, into the duodenum, the first part of the small intestine. It typically takes me several hours to work through an entire meal, and if it's really big or fatty, I have to put in overtime.

The only time I ever stop is when your brain releases the stress hormone cortisol. That "fight-or-flight" response either shuts down digestion completely, making me feel full of butterflies, or speeds it up to the point that you feel sick. That's what stress will do to you, though.

When I'm completely empty, you'll feel those contractions as hunger pangs, which I jump-start by releasing ghrelin into your bloodstream. Your brain sends me signals to make me secrete this hormone, known as the "hunger hormone."

You might hear those contractions, too—an empty stomach amplifies the rumbles. The other

IS YOUR BELLY GENDER-BIASED?

WHEN IT COMES TO STOMACH WOES, MEN AND WOMEN AREN'T ALWAYS ON THE SAME TRACT

➤ Women usually are more sensitive than men to bitter and sweet flavors.

➤ Our esophageal sphincter (the muscle that keeps food and digestive juices in the stomach) squeezes shut with more force than men's does. A similar muscle that protects the windpipe also tightens more, which may explain why women get that "lump in the throat" more often than guys do—or more often than they'll admit to, anyway.

➤ Women secrete less stomach acid and tend to have fewer acid-related stomach ulcers than men.

➤ Women generally suffer less esophageal damage from heartburn than men do.

➤ Women report nausea, bloating, tummy pain, and burping more often than men.

➤ Women suffer from irritable bowel syndrome (IBS) two to six times as often as men. This may be because women are normally more sensitive to irritants of the GI tract: In IBS, the patient reacts to irritants such as increased gas in the gut.

TOTAL FITNESS GUIDE 2009

W|H

noises I make are just normal digestion. I'll sound off for 10 to 20 minutes while I'm digesting food, and then again every 1 to 2 hours until you down your next meal. Sorry I don't always have the best timing (I forgot you had that big presentation at work last week). But I'm not alone in the noisemaking; your small intestines get rowdy too: As food makes its way to the large intestine, it pushes air and liquid around in your bowels, and that causes all those gurgling sounds.

If you really want me to quiet down, steer clear of the break room on Krispy Kreme days. Your brain releases ghrelin to tip me off the second you see or smell food, so I can get my juices flowing in

TUMMY TRIVIA

Think your stomach acts weird? Check out the digestive gymnastics accomplished by other members of the animal kingdom. Better yet, try to match each animal to its dumb tummy trick.

1. Can turn its stomach inside out

2. Vomits its stomach, wipes off the dangling contents, and then swallows the organ back down again

3. Has been found with more than 200 crabs in its stomach

4. Has a four-chambered stomach

5. Once had a 10-pound hairball removed from its stomach

6. Has two stomachs: one for its own food and another for food to be shared with others

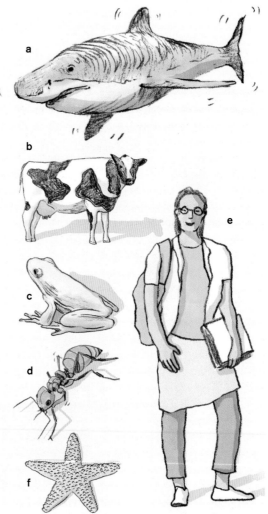

Answers: 1: f; 2: c; 3: a; 4: b; 5: e (surprise—it actually happened last year to an 18-year-old woman); 6: d

preparation. And I especially like sugar. In fact, I have some of the same sweet-detecting proteins that are in your tongue. I use them to help regulate insulin production and appetite. I can't exactly "taste" sugar the same way your tongue does, but sweetness does make me rev up the release of hormones that make you feel happy.

And please remember: While you might notice the difference between diet and regular, I can't. I'll react to artificial sweeteners as if they're the real thing: by wanting more. That's why every time you down a Diet Coke, you get a hankering for a brownie.

When you eat too much, I definitely feel it. I try to help kick-start the release of leptin, the hormone that tells you you're full and induces nausea. It's my way of saying "Stop!" So give me a chance to say it before you wolf down seconds. A third of what you eat is processed in about 20 minutes, so if you take the time to chew and enjoy your meal, you'll push yourself away from the table before you overdo it. That's good, because too many supersize meals can desensitize my stretch receptors, the ones that let your brain know I'm maxed out, and then it'll take a lot more food to make me feel full next time.

The good news is that unlike your boss, I respond well to sensitivity training. Eat smaller meals for a while, and I'll get used to more reasonable portions again and feel full on less food. Just don't cut back too far. I'm no fan of being empty, and when you don't feed me enough, I have no choice but to let loose more ghrelin. That can send you running for the junk-food aisle— and neither of us wants that. Let's strike a

bargain: Don't let me get empty, and I'll go easy on the "Feed me, Seymour" dramatics. Just keep small, healthy meals coming throughout the day so I stay busy.

You can help by choosing foods that take me longer to digest. That includes protein: fish, chicken breast, lean beef, eggs, and skim milk. Fiber-filled foods, especially those mixed with water, like brown rice and oatmeal, tend to stick around a while too. In a pinch, other carbs will do, though I generally go through them a lot faster. They subdue ghrelin, but only temporarily—and when it bounces back, it's with a vengeance, making you more ravenous than you were before you ate. Even worse is overloading on fats. They are the least efficient at suppressing ghrelin, so try to avoid

giving me a whole lot of them on a regular basis, unless you want to hear me grumble about it.

Unfortunately, I stink at math, so it's up to you to count calories. It's all the same to me, whether you fill me up with french fries or salad, because I react to volume, not density. I don't know how much fat is in those fries, but I do know they aren't going to keep me happy for as long as, say, some fresh fruit.

And while we're on the subject, I know you've been thinking about Alli, that over-the-counter diet aid. Well, let me make up your mind for you: Fat substitutes and fat-blockers, including olestra-filled foods like Wow potato chips and Alli, go right through me. Mess with them and you may be able to finish *War and Peace* on the john. These products work by preventing enzymes from breaking down fat, so it gets eliminated with other waste instead of ending up on your thighs. But urgent bowel movements, diarrhea, and gas with horrible oily spotting come with the territory. I think you've got better things to do with your time.

Well, thanks for listening. I think we make a pretty good team, you and I. I'll keep expanding to meet your needs, sterilizing your grub, and churning it into your intestines if you keep me full of protein and fiber, stop eating when I'm full, and steer clear of crazy fad diets. Maybe this year we can even enjoy swimsuit season together.

Oh, and if you don't mind, grab a snack soon. It's getting a little lonely down here.

Hey bee-atch, you call this breakfast!?

Sources: David E. Cummings, M.D., professor of medicine in the division of metabolism, endocrinology, and nutrition at the University of Washington; William Chey, M.D., professor of medicine in the division of gastroenterology at the University of Michigan Health System; Elizabeth Somer, M.A., R.D., the author of 10 Habits That Mess Up a Woman's Diet; Brian Wansink, Ph.D., director of the Cornell University Food and Brand Lab and the author of Mindless Eating *(mindlesseating. org) and* Why We Eat More Than We Think.

TRANSIT TIME

You know those moments, usually after a big, greasy meal, when it feels as if your food is just sitting in your stomach? Sometimes it actually is. Food can take about 6 to 8 hours to pass through your stomach and small intestines, and on average, it takes anywhere from 1 to 3 days to pass through your whole digestive system. Here's where some common foods stack up in the race through your insides:

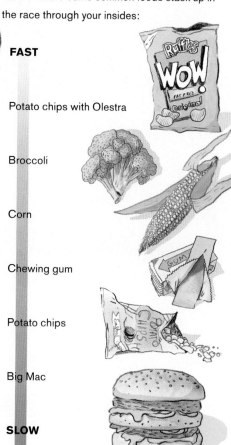

FAST

Potato chips with Olestra

Broccoli

Corn

Chewing gum

Potato chips

Big Mac

SLOW

wbe

CHAPTER TWENTY-FOUR

ACCELERATE THE BURN

FIRE UP YOUR METABOLISM WITH THE *WH* 20-MINUTE WORKOUT SERIES.

BY JENNY EVERETT

NEED A REASON TO TACKLE THE workout that follows? These moves, from exercise physiologist and *WH* columnist Amy Dixon, will increase the rate at which you burn calories by up to 13 percent. The key to this kind of caloric demolition is a type of workout called a superset, in which you do two moves back to back with zero rest. It will hurt—but you won't be sorry. Because with supersets, you'll not only get that initial (and insane!) metabolic spike, but according to a study from Colorado State University, you'll continue to burn calories at a higher rate for up to 16 hours after you leave the gym. How's that for motivation?

Recover Right

Proper recovery is key to feeling fab and staying injury-free. Follow these rules from John Berardi, Ph.D., president and founder of Precision Nutrition.

During Your Workout

Sip an energy drink. Go for one with a 2-to-1 ratio of carbs to protein: any product that has about 24 grams of carbs and 12 grams of protein. Berardi likes half a serving of Biotest Surge Recovery, a powder that you mix with water ($30 for 16 servings, biotest.net). Can't find a brand your taste buds can tolerate? Try 6 to 8 ounces of Gatorade mixed with a scoop of whey protein powder.

Postworkout

Do 15 minutes of low-impact cardio, then eat ASAP. "Your blood sugar levels are low, so you may feel agitated," Berardi says. That's your body saying "Feed me. Now!" For a quick fix, order this at your smoothie bar: 1 to 2 cups of skim or soy milk, 1 to 2 cups of frozen fruit, and a scoop each of whey protein and green powder. (The latter is packed with recovery-aiding antioxidants.)

The Next Day

Light activity will keep your muscles from tightening up. Walking the dog, taking a yoga class, or chasing your niece at the playground are all legit options.

Fry Fat

INCINERATE UP TO 400 CALORIES IN 20 MINUTES Burn more by doing two moves back to back with no rest in between. Complete this workout twice a week, opting for a weight at which you can barely eke out the last rep of your final set with perfect form.

WORKOUTS BY AMY DIXON

LEAPFROG

WORKS ENTIRE LOWER BODY AND HEART

Stand facing a 12- to 18-inch step. With your feet hip-width apart, bend slightly at your knees and jump up onto the step (A). Land quietly, letting your heels hit first and bending your knees as you land (B). Push off with your heels and jump back down, landing softly, heel to toe (C). Continue for 1 minute.

A

B

C

BOSU BURPIE PUSHUP

WORKS CHEST AND CORE

Place a BOSU on the floor, dome side down, and stand facing it. With your feet hip-width apart, squat, lean forward, and grab the sides of the BOSU (A). Jump your feet back into plank position and straighten your arms. Brace your abs and do a pushup (B). Jump back into a squat, then stand. That's 1 rep. Do 12 to 15.

Superset 1

Alternate between sets of the Leapfrog (page 207) and BOSU Burpie Pushup. Complete three sets of each.

A

B

POWER KNEE TAP 'N' TOUCH

WORKS ENTIRE LOWER BODY AND HEART

Stand alongside a 12-inch-high bench. Step up with
your left foot; then, swinging your left arm to help
propel your body, jump up and bring your right thigh
to hip height (A). Land so both feet are on the bench,
knees slightly bent. Immediately step your right foot
down to the floor, and with your left foot, take a giant
step behind you and sink into a lunge. Place your left
hand next to your right foot (B). Do the sequence for
30 seconds, then repeat on the other side. That's one
set.

A

B

ON-GUARD LUNGES

WORKS SHOULDERS, GLUTES,
AND ALL THE THIGH MUSCLES

Grab a pair of 5- to 10-pound dumbbells; lunge
forward with your left foot. Place your right hand on
your hip and raise your left arm in front of you at
shoulder height, pointing the weight like a sword (A).
Step back to center. Lunge out to the left, place your
right hand on your hip, and raise your left arm out to
the side at shoulder height (B). That's 1 rep. Do 8 to
10 reps and then do the moves on the opposite side.
That's one set.

Superset 2

*Alternate between sets of the Power Knee Tap 'n'
Touch (page 209) and On-Guard Lunges. Complete
three sets of each.*

A

B

TRICEP DIP AND REACH

WORKS TRICEPS AND CORE

Sit on the floor with your knees slightly bent and your back as close as you can get it to a 12-inch-high step. Grab the edge of the step with your hands slightly more than hip-width apart. Push your heels into the floor as you straighten your arms. Perform a dip (A). Straighten your arms, then reach your left arm straight out in front of your body at shoulder height while lifting your right leg (B). Hold for a few seconds, then repeat, lifting the opposite arm and leg. That's 1 rep. Do 12 to 15.

A

B

CLIMB THE MOUNTAIN

WORKS SHOULDERS, CHEST, CORE,
AND LOWER BODY

Get into plank position with your hands shoulder-width apart on a 12-inch-high step (A). Step forward to the front of the bench with your right foot, keeping your left leg straight and your right thigh parallel to the floor (B). With your hands on the step, jump, switch legs in the air, and land with your right leg straight behind you and your left leg bent. Continue hopping to switch legs for 1 minute. That's one set.

Superset 3

Alternate between sets of Tricep Dip and Reach (page 211) and Climb the Mountain. Complete three sets of each.

A

B

PLANK ROW AND LEG LIFT

WORKS BACK, CORE, AND GLUTES

Place a pair of 5- to 10-pound dumbbells shoulder-width apart on a 12-inch-high step. Get in plank position with your hands on the dumbbells (A). In one motion, lift the right dumbbell until your elbow passes your torso and raise your left leg to hip height (B). Lower and repeat with the opposite arm and leg. That's 1 rep. Do 12 to 15.

Superset 4

This move is so tough you don't need to superset it. You'll know what we mean when you try it!

A

B

W|H

■ PART SIX

maintenance

Once you get the fit, healthy body you've always wanted, you'll need strategies to keep it that way. Everything from picking the right workout gear and rehabbing your feet to spotting a fitness or nutrition myth when you see it is covered in this last piece of the *Women's Health Total Fitness Guide*.

216

CHAPTER TWENTY-FIVE

THE RIGHT STUFF

10 PIECES OF GEAR EVERY WOMAN—YES, EVEN NONJOCKS—SHOULD OWN

BY DIMITY McDOWELL

WHEN IT COMES TO FITNESS GEAR, fads have an annoying way of trumping function (witness: that thigh gizmo in your closet). But in your quest for fun-filled weekends—and a double-take bod—you need stuff that performs day in and day out. So we asked 200 *WH* readers what types of gear (from water bottles to golf clubs) are most essential to their active lifestyles, then compiled the top 10 and tracked down the best new item in each category. Invest in these must-haves—we promise they'll never end up in your I-can't-believe-I-own-that pile.

Lightweight, Waterproof Jacket

OUR PICK Weighing in at a gossamerlike 7.1 ounces, The North Face Diad ($199, thenorthface.com) stuffs easily into a small pocket, but once you shake her out, she's all business. With sealed seams (a waterproof must), three pockets, and Velcro cuffs, this "Teflon Don" protects you from everything Ma N. tosses your way.

What to Look For

Nylon covered with a waterproof coating is the fabric of choice for most lightweight jackets. For maximum AC, look for pit zips and mesh-lined pockets, which allow air to circulate and wick away sweat.

Does-It-All Running Shoe

OUR PICK The Brooks Glycerin 6 ($120, brooks running.com) is designed to delight most any foot. Its midsole has up to 40 percent more cushioning than other running shoes, and it has gel-like balloons under the forefoot and heel that absorb shock. A roomy toe box completes the fab fit.

What to Look For

A very cush fit. You should be able to wiggle your toes and have about a thumb's width of room between your longest toe and the end of the shoe, especially if you're a trail runner or climb a lot, so your toes don't jam to the front on the downhills, says John O'Neill, manager of the Colorado Running Company in Colorado Springs.

WH readers say running shoes are the No. 1 piece of gear they need to be fit.

W|H

Sweet Shades

OUR PICK The Oakley Endure (from $155, oakley
.com), the company's first stab at sports shades specifically for women, is spot-on: The lenses not only
reflect all evil rays but also repel water, so rain
won't muck them up. And the grippy nose and ear
stays keep the specs in place no matter how much
you sweat.

What to Look For

Shatterproof lenses that protect you from 100 percent of UVA and UVB rays. They should be snug
enough to stay on when you bend down to tie your
laces (but not so tight that they pinch).

Spine-Friendly Daypack

OUR PICK With a wide and comfy belt, Mammut's
Energise Duo pack ($139, mammutusa.com) dis-
tributes weight gently. Plentiful pockets hold everything from maps to hydration bladders, and a rear
mesh panel presses the pack away from your back
to help wick away sweat.

What to Look For

A hip belt to direct weight off your spine and shoulders (yes, it can look dorky, but you won't care come
mile 6 up a mountain). "If you're under 5 foot 10,
consider a woman-specific pack," says Alex Gil-
man, a product trainer at REI in Fairfax, Virginia.
"The back is shorter and the shoulder straps are
narrower than on a unisex pack."

Light, Nontoxic Water Bottle

OUR PICK Holding a little over 32 ounces of water, the Sigg Think Green aluminum bottle ($25, mysigg.com) practices the environmental awareness it preaches. After hundreds of uses, it still won't leach any chemicals. If you're a cyclist or runner and want something to fit in your hand or bottle cage, go for one of their 0.75-liter versions ($20).

What to Look For

Anything but polycarbonate plastic, which is indicated by a number "7" in a triangle on the bottom. Although the jury is still out on their safety, bottles made of this stuff contain bisphenol A, which some studies indicate can mess with estrogen levels. We'll play it safe, thanks.

Gym Bag That Doesn't Scream "Jock!"

OUR PICK With as many pockets as Katie Couric's reporting-from-a-war-zone vest, the Sherpani Blaze ($65, sherpanipacks.com) has spots for your water bottle, deodorant, and gym shoes, and even a fleece-lined pocket for scratch-free sunglasses stowage. Carry it as a duffel or pull out the tuckaway shoulder straps and wear it as a backpack.

What to Look For

Something that isn't black, rectangular, and plastered with an obnoxious logo. Even better: plenty of small pockets and a waterproof pouch to separate wet and dry items—handy if you soak through sports bras.

Durable Exercise Band

OUR PICK With four narrow tubes braided together, snap-resistant Spri SportCords (from $25, spriproducts.com) come in five resistance levels. Beginners should pick up a level two for upper-body work and a three for total-body; more regular exercisers should go for a three and a four.

What to Look For

Comfy handles and a rugged design. Gregory Florez, CEO of FitAdvisor Health Coaching Services in Salt Lake City, recommends buying two bands: a lighter one for upper-body buffing and a heavy-resistance one for full-body moves.

Barely There Music Player

OUR PICK The SanDisk Sansa Clip ($60, shopsansa.com). The size of a Tic Tac box, this player has 2 GB of storage (enough for about 500 tunes) and clips onto your clothing. Browsing tracks is a snap, and a built-in FM transmitter can even pick up channels on the TV at your gym.

What to Look For

Flash memory (a traditional hard drive is less durable), minimal buttons to fuss with, and one or two gigs of storage, says Tracy Wilson, a technology writer for the website howstuffworks .com. You also should be able to attach it securely to your body, and it shouldn't break the bank (you'll be tossing it into a gym bag, after all).

Anti-Chafing Bike Short

OUR PICK Zoot Sports CycleFit BioWrap Shorts ($80, zootsports.com) make any bike seat feel like a Caddy. What's more, they eliminate sausage leg with hems that keep your shorts in place without cutting off your blood supply.

What to Look For

Ample padding where it counts most. The chamois (rhymes with whammy) should be no thicker than a deck of cards, says Jennifer Skorcz, a former bike mechanic and owner of Cycling Essentials in Colorado Springs.

Tip: Go commando in the shorts—"Not even a thong," Skorcz says—and try Ozone Protect chamois cream ($20, worldcycling.com).

A Bicycle Fit for You

OUR PICK The Giant OCR AOW ($1,800, giant forwomen.com for stores) offers a more upright position than other road bikes and accommodates wider hips, narrower shoulders, smaller hands, and other anatomical specs of the female body. It may seem pricey, but it's such a comfy ride, you'll want to keep it forever.

Made of stiff aluminum (which translates your pedal prowess directly into speed) and lightweight, bump-dampening carbon fiber, this 20-speed horse has gears that make climbing a cinch, while its chick-specific design means descending is way less shriek-provoking because your weight is distributed evenly. (Giant also makes the woman-specific OCR A1W, with slightly less-fancy parts, for $1,400.)

What to Look For

A ride you can sit on for 3 hours, no prob. When picking a road bike, "pay attention to your reach, or the extension from your hips to your hands," Skorcz says. Men typically have longer arms and torsos than women, so riding a guy's bike would stretch you out, making it hard to react safely on the fly. Also—shocker—the typical female pelvis is wider than the male counterpart, so we need a wider, shorter saddle. General rule: If you're under 5' 10", shop for a woman-specific bike.

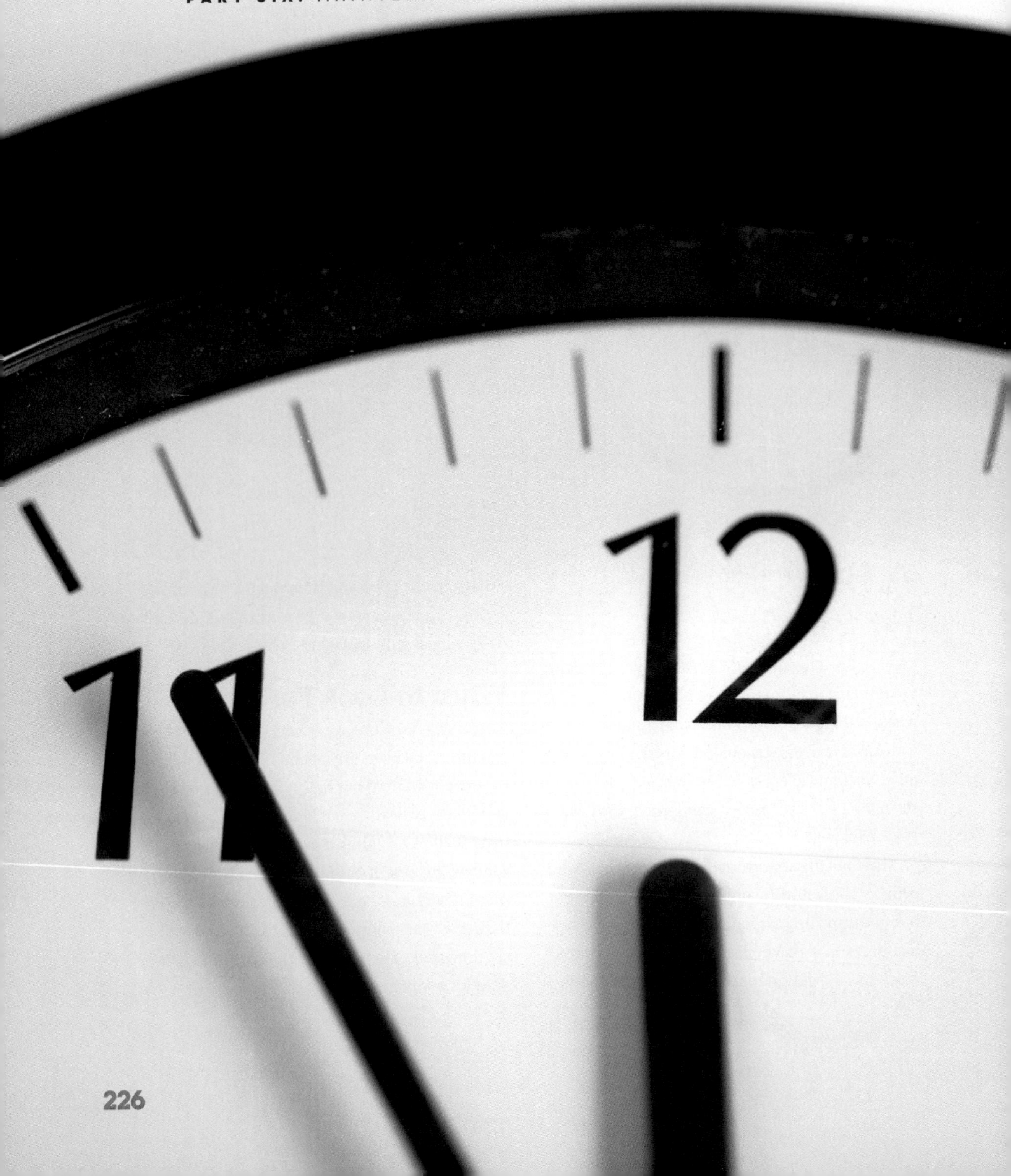
12
11

CHAPTER TWENTY-SIX

GOT A MINUTE?

RATCHET UP POINTS FOR HEALTHY BEHAVIOR WITH THESE 60-SECOND FIXES.

BY LAURIE McLAUGHLIN; ADDITIONAL REPORTING BY KATHLEEN PENNEPACKER

TOTAL FITNESS GUIDE 2009

W|H

ADD UP ALL THE THINGS you're supposed to do every day to stay healthy (the sleeping, the sweating, the veggie steaming, the Sudoku-solving) and it can feel like a full-time job. But studies show you can reap major body benefits—whether you double the calories you burn in a workout or reduce your risk of cancer—in 60 seconds or less. That should leave plenty of time for Netflix, YouTube, Zappos . . . you know, the important stuff.

When You're at the Drugstore

THE CHANGE: Read the fine print on sunscreen labels.

THE BENEFIT: Better SPF protection. A recent test of sunscreen products found that 83 percent of them don't provide adequate sun protection. To guard against both UVA and UVB rays, look for products that contain zinc (or zinc oxide) and titanium (or titanium dioxide).

On Your Way Home from Work

THE CHANGE: Stop by the florist.

THE BENEFIT: Less grouchiness the next morning. New research from Harvard University shows that even people who say they're not "morning people" report feeling happier and more energetic after looking at flowers first thing in the a.m.

When You First Get to Work

THE CHANGE: Check out a funny website.

THE BENEFIT: Fewer colds. Instead of starting your day with office e-mail, try a gutbuster from a site like Will Ferrell and co.'s funnyordie.com. Research suggests that a moment of mirth increases the body's secretion of immune-boosting growth hormones and endorphins.

When You Skin Your Knee

THE CHANGE: Dab some honey on it.

THE BENEFIT: Fewer Band-Aids required. A study in the *International Journal of Clinical Practice* shows that natural disinfectants in honey can speed healing, reduce the risk of infection, and

soothe pain. Just apply a thin layer over small cuts and scrapes.

When You're Having Your Annual Check-Up

THE CHANGE: Tackle the tough stuff first.

THE BENEFIT: A better relationship with your doctor. Research shows that patients who bring up difficult issues at the start of an appointment are more likely to be satisfied with the visit and to adhere to their M.D.'s recommendations.

When You Want a Snack

THE CHANGE: Pop pistachios.

THE BENEFIT: Improved cholesterol levels. In research at the Inova Fairfax Hospital in Falls Church, Virginia, people who ate 2 to 3 ounces of unsalted pistachios a day for 4 weeks raised their HDL cholesterol (the good kind) by 6 percent. Buy them preshelled to save your nails, too.

During a DIY Pedi

THE CHANGE: Examine your feet.

THE BENEFIT: Early skin cancer detection. Melanoma can develop even in places that don't see much sun. The three most common on the feet: the soles, between the toes, and around or under the toenails. See a doc if you notice spots that are new or asymmetrical or that change in size, color, or thickness.

When You're Yawning at 3 p.m.

THE CHANGE: Choose coffee over cola.

THE BENEFIT: Reduced diabetes risk. Coffee has fewer cals and more antioxidants than most sodas—and a Finnish study found that folks who drank three to six cups per day were 50 percent less likely to develop type 2 diabetes than those who sipped two cups or less.

During the Week Before Your Period

THE CHANGE: Order a glass of wine with dinner.

THE BENEFIT: Less PMS. The Study of Women's Health across the Nation recently linked moderate alcohol consumption (about one drink per day) to fewer preperiod mood changes and headaches.

When You're Making Burritos for Dinner

THE CHANGE: Swap in a blue tortilla for a white one.

THE BENEFIT: Fewer late-night hunger pangs. Scientists in Mexico recently found that blue tortillas contain 20 percent more hunger-satisfying protein and 16 percent less blood-sugar-spiking starch than white ones.

When You're Craving a Cigarette

THE CHANGE: Drink milk.

THE BENEFIT: Less-satisfying smoke breaks. In a recent survey of smokers from Duke University, nearly 20 percent agreed that milk makes cigarettes taste bad. "Your brain can eventually connect the taste of milk with a decreased desire to smoke," says lead researcher Joseph McClernon, Ph.D.

When You're Waiting for the Weight Machine at the Gym

THE CHANGE: Skip rope.

THE BENEFIT: Megacalorie frying. "Jumping rope for 1 minute and then resting for 1 minute between sets of weight-training exercises can nearly double the calories you burn," says Patrick Murphy, a personal trainer in Los Angeles.

W|H

230

CHAPTER TWENTY-SEVEN

USELESS
ADVICE

THEY SAY YOU SHOULD BANISH LATE-NIGHT MEALS, SLAVE OVER OLD-FASHIONED OATMEAL, AND STOP AFTER ONE BITE OF DESSERT. OBVIOUSLY, "THEY" DON'T LIVE IN THE REAL WORLD.

BY KATE ASHFORD CARPENTER

MOST OF THE TIME, nutritionists and dietitians are full of brilliant ideas that help you eat healthier, stay slimmer, and live longer. But every once in a while, food gurus forget that the rest of us have limited time, funds, and willpower. That's when they spit out wonky bits of wisdom like "Ask your waiter to wrap half your entrée before you start eating." Yeah, he'd be happy to—right after he sticks his thumb in your salade Nicoise. We collected seven of the hardest-to-swallow expert suggestions and replaced them with equally healthy tips that a normal person can actually use. Because unless your name is Jessica Seinfeld, you're not going to spend every second fretting about what goes on your plate.

THE ADVICE: Chug eight glasses of water a day.

WHY IT'S USELESS: Peeing every 20 minutes seriously interferes with life.

THE REAL DEAL: Believe it or not, the eight-glass quota isn't etched in stone. Yes, we need to be well hydrated, but if your urine is clear or close to it, you're probably getting enough fluids. If your No. 1 is neon yellow, lighten things up by adding one or two glasses a day. Once your body adjusts to getting more fluid (and you don't have to run to the can every 10 minutes), add another, says Karen Benzinger, R.D., a dietary consultant in Chicago who specializes in health care. And don't forget that all liquids—including tea, juice, even the tonic in your vodka drink—help keep your body sufficiently saturated.

THE ADVICE: Don't drink juice—it's a sugar bomb.

WHY IT'S USELESS: Juice is a breakfast staple, and it's essential for smoothies.

THE REAL DEAL: There's a big difference between 100 percent juice and a bottle of sugar water with a few cranberries squeezed into it. Yes, juice has a lot of the sweet stuff, but a 6-ounce glass of 100 percent juice also counts as a full serving of fruit and delivers many of the same vitamins and antioxidants, making it worth the occasional sugar rush, says Jessica Ganzer, R.D., owner of Ganzer Wellness Consulting in Arlington, Virginia. And it can be the easiest way to get a superfood: Drinking 100 percent pomegranate juice is easy; picking apart a real pomegranate, not so much. As long as you drink 100 percent

juice (from concentrate is fine) and limit yourself to one 6- to 8-ounce glass a day, you're not breaking any rules of good nutrition. If you're seriously cutting back on calories or carbs, try Tropicana's Light 'n Healthy line; a serving has about half the sugar (10 grams) and calories (50) of normal juice.

THE ADVICE: Shut the kitchen down after 7 p.m. to prevent weight gain.

WHY IT'S USELESS: After a long day at the office and a trip to the gym, you either eat dinner at 9:30 or starve.

THE REAL DEAL: The no-food-right-before-bed rule was meant for the nighttime nosher who mindlessly wolfs down a bag of Oreos while watching *CSI: Miami*. If you get home long after dark, a late dinner is perfectly fine. A calorie is a calorie, no matter what time you eat it, according to Katie Clark, R.D., M.P.H., assistant professor of family health care nursing at the University of California, San Francisco. But do keep your evening meal light—along the lines of a chicken breast, steamed broccoli, and brown rice. Too much chow will keep you up at night: To break down all that food, your gut has to churn like a cement truck.

THE ADVICE: Simmer steel-cut oatmeal instead of nuking the instant kind.

WHY IT'S USELESS: The only way we have time for breakfast is if making breakfast doesn't take any time.

THE REAL DEAL: The pros push this tip because people usually eat flavored instant oatmeal, which comes with up to a whopping 13 grams of sugar per 43-gram packet—compared with 1 gram or less of sweetness in the steel-cut stuff. And steel-cut oats are less processed than the rolled oats used in the just-add-water variety, so they take longer to digest (this keeps your blood sugar nice and steady, helping you avoid mood swings and hunger pangs). That said, instant oatmeal still uses whole grain oats (they're just mashed a bit more), so it comes with most of the same health benefits. One of these is the cholesterol-lowering, hunger-satisfying soluble fiber beta-glucan: It turns gummy when it hits your GI tract, binds with cholesterol, and drags it out. "I'd rather my clients eat 1-minute oatmeal than no oatmeal at all," Ganzer says. If you find unsweet-

ened oatmeal about as appetizing as paste, combine half a packet of the flavored kind with half a packet of plain. Or consider Quaker Oatmeal's Weight Control flavored instants, which pack even more fiber than steel-cut oats (6 grams per packet) and keep sugar down to 1 gram.

THE ADVICE: If you must drink while you diet, order a white-wine spritzer.

WHY IT'S USELESS: Despite the dainty name, it tastes just like what it is: watered-down wine.

THE REAL DEAL: There's no weight-loss magic in a spritzer, a cup of wine diluted with calorie-free carbonated water. It's just another portion-control trick that trims your total calorie intake, Clark says.

If you balk at the idea of outdated cocktails or weak-tasting grape juice, slowly sipping a glass of water between rounds of pinot grigio accomplishes the same goal.

THE ADVICE: Put half your entrée in a to-go box before you start to eat.

WHY IT'S USELESS: You know you have portion-control issues, but that doesn't mean you want everyone else at your table to know it too.

THE REAL DEAL: A better way to cut back on restaurant binging is to pretend the breadbasket is sprinkled with cyanide and to double up on veggie sides instead of ordering fries. Also effective: putting your fork down between bites, which gives your stomach and brain time to register that you're full (which takes about 20 minutes). Once your gauge hits "F," ask the waiter to box up the rest of your food right away so you won't keep nibbling, Benzinger says.

THE ADVICE: Have just one bite of dessert.

WHY IT'S USELESS: That's like telling an addict to have just a little crack.

THE REAL DEAL: Eating chocolate cake is like watching *Keeping Up with the Kardashians:* There's nothing right about it, so just revel in how deliciously wrong it is. A smarter strategy: Before you begin the debauchery, plan for the extra calories—skip the appetizer, the bread, or (ouch) the booze. "If the dessert is really that good, it's worth the sacrifice," Benzinger says.

CHAPTER TWENTY-EIGHT

DOGGY DAY CARE

ERASE THE AGONY OF THE FEET WITH THESE ANKLES-DOWN STRENGTHENERS.

CONSIDERING THAT EACH OF YOUR FEET is made up of 33 joints, more than 100 ligaments, and 26 bones, they deserve more than just a pedicure. "If they're not strong and properly aligned, the repercussions will echo through your body," says Erika Bloom, owner of Erika Bloom Pilates Plus in New York City. Do this tootsie workout twice a week. And as you learn to lift your arches, spread your toes, and center your weight over your entire foot, you'll help all your muscles move better. "Your spine will stack as it should, your core will engage, and your posture will improve immediately," says Bloom.

The Moves

CATERPILLAR

STRENGTHENS ARCHES

Lie on your back with your feet flat on the floor, hip-distance apart and 2 feet from your butt. Lift both arches and draw your toes toward your heels. Then relax the arches and slide your heels toward your glutes and flatten your feet. Repeat the sequence until your heels nearly reach your glutes. Repeat in reverse: arches up, heels toward toes, toes spread forward as arches flatten. Continue until you're where you started. That's one set. Do three.

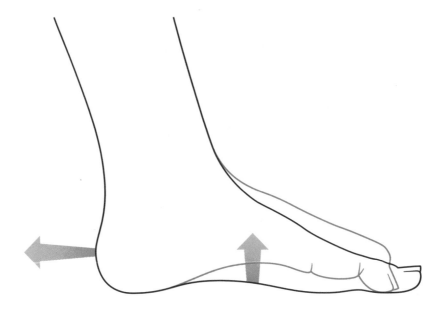

WINDSHIELD WIPER

IMPROVES ANKLE STABILITY,
STRENGTHENS ENTIRE FOOT

Lie on your back with your knees bent and your feet
flat on the floor, hip-distance apart and 2 feet from
your butt. Lift your toes so only your heels are on the
floor and your feet are flexed. From heel to toe, slowly
roll your feet to the floor and lift your heels until only
your pointed toes are on the floor. That's 1 rep.
Repeat 10 times.

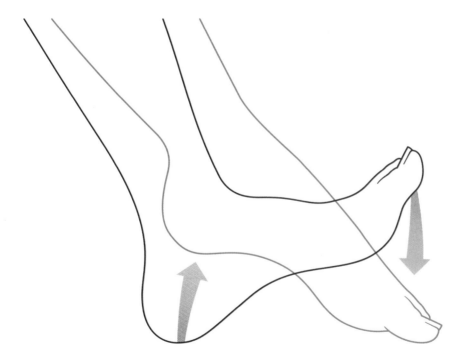

WING AND SICKLE

STRENGTHENS ANKLE,
PROMOTES CORRECT GAIT

Lie on your back with your feet flat on the floor, hip-
distance apart and 2 feet from your butt. Roll your feet
onto their inside edges, keeping the insides of your
big toes on the ground (your feet will resemble
wings). Then roll your feet to their outer edges so the
outsides of your pinkies and heels are on the floor.
Repeat, slowly walking your feet away from each
other until they're 2 to 3 feet apart, then walk them
back together. That's one set. Do three.

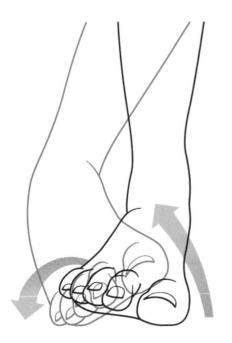
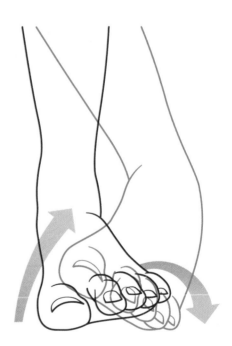

THE ROUND KNOT

STRETCHES FOOT LIGAMENTS, AIDS ALIGNMENT

Sit on the floor with your legs extended in front of you.
Bend your left knee 90 degrees and place the outside
of your left calf on top of your right thigh. Interlace your
right fingertips with your left toes. Spreading your
fingers, inch them forward until your toes are on the
webbing between your fingers. Close your hand and,
letting the foot totally relax, make large circles with
your feet. Do six in one direction and six in the other,
then switch feet.

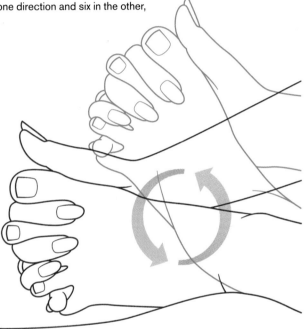

WTF IS ... DOMS?!

It stands for Delayed Onset Muscle Soreness, which is what you have when you feel really freaking sore
about 24 hours after a tough workout. But it is a good excuse for a rubdown. A recent study published in
the *Journal of Athletic Training* found that a massage can reduce DOMS symptoms by up to 30 percent.
Visit amtamassage.org to find a certified massage therapist.

CHAPTER TWENTY-NINE

BONUS
RECIPES

NOWING THE RIGHT FOODS TO EAT is just as important as having a fool-proof fitness plan. That's why we've gathered together some all-star recipes—comfort foods included—for meals that will perfectly complement any fitness plan. Not only are these dishes delicious, they're healthful and will keep your body full of energy and fuel to get the most from our workouts.

ASIAN PORK MEATBALLS ON SHREDDED VEGETABLES

Prep Time: 15 minutes; Cook Time: 10 minutes; Total Time: 25 minutes

This sophisticated appetizer is a delicious first course for a special dinner.

Meatballs

- 1 medium cucumber, shredded
- 1 medium carrot, shredded
- 1 pound ground lean pork
- 3 pieces water chestnut, finely chopped
- 1 tablespoon finely chopped scallion
- 2 tablespoons reduced-sodium soy sauce
- 2 large eggs
- $\frac{1}{4}$ teaspoon ground black pepper
- $\frac{1}{4}$ cup panko bread crumbs

Dipping Sauce

- 3 tablespoons reduced-sodium soy sauce
- 1 tablespoon canola oil
- 1 teaspoon toasted sesame oil
- 1 scallion, sliced
- $\frac{1}{2}$ teaspoon grated fresh ginger

Preheat the oven to 375°F.

To prepare the meatballs: In a small bowl, combine the cucumber and carrot. Set aside. In a food processor fitted with a metal blade, combine the pork, water chestnut, scallion, soy sauce, eggs, pepper, and bread crumbs. Pulse several times just to combine.

With a melon baller or fingers, shape the meat mixture into balls and place on a baking sheet. Bake for 10 minutes, turning meatballs once, until the pork is no longer pink and the juices run clear.

To prepare the dipping sauce: While the meatballs are baking, in a small bowl, combine the soy sauce, canola oil, sesame oil, scallion, and ginger. Stir to mix. Set aside.

Arrange the reserved cucumber-carrot mixture in small mounds on a serving plate. Arrange the meatballs around the vegetables. Drizzle with a small amount of the sauce. Serve the remaining sauce on the side.

MAKES 8 SERVINGS

PER SERVING: 136 calories, 15 g protein, 6 g carbohydrates, 6 g fat (1.5 g saturated), 90 mg cholesterol, 1 g fiber, 411 mg sodium

PORTOBELLO SANDWICH

Prep Time: 5 minutes; Cook Time: 15 minutes; Total Time: 20 minutes

This sandwich is so tasty and succulent that you won't miss the meat.

1 teaspoon olive oil

1 onion slice, ¼" thick

¼ red bell pepper, cut into thick strips

1 medium portobello mushroom cap
Salt

1 slice reduced-fat provolone cheese

1 teaspoon prepared pesto

1 focaccia roll or 1"–2" slice focaccia bread
(about 2 ounces), split in half horizontally

1 lettuce leaf

1 slice tomato

PER SERVING: 302 calories, 12 g protein, 39 g carbohydrates, 12 g fat (3 g saturated), 12 mg cholesterol, 3 g fiber, 650 mg sodium

Preheat the oven to 400°F.

In a nonstick skillet over medium heat, warm the oil. Add the onion and bell pepper. Cook, tossing occasionally, for about 5 minutes, or until softened. Scrape the vegetables to the side. Place the mushroom in the pan, top side up. Cook for about 2 minutes. Turn over and cook for 2 minutes more, or until softened. Season the mushroom cap and vegetables lightly with salt.

Transfer the mushroom to a baking pan or piece of heavy aluminum foil. Top with the onion, pepper, and cheese. Bake for 5 minutes, or until the cheese bubbles.

Meanwhile, spread the pesto on both sides of the roll or bread. Transfer the mushroom, onion, and pepper to the bottom bun. Top with lettuce, tomato, and top bun. Slice in half and serve.

MAKES 1 SERVING

TUNA YACHTS

Prep Time: 5 minutes; Cook Time: none; Total Time: 5 minutes

Change your snacking from chips and ice cream to a better choice.

- 1 can (6 ounces) albacore tuna in water, drained
- 1 hard-cooked egg, chopped
- 1 tablespoon finely chopped red onion
- 1 tablespoon finely chopped celery
- 2 tablespoons low-fat mayonnaise
- 1/4 teaspoon salt
- Ground black pepper
- 1 head Belgian endive

In a bowl, combine the tuna, egg, onion, celery, mayonnaise, salt, and pepper. Separate the endive leaves and arrange on a platter. Fill each leaf with some of the tuna salad.

MAKES 12 SERVINGS

PER SERVING: 30 calories, 4 g protein, 1 g carbohydrates, 1 g fat (0.5 g saturated), 24 mg cholesterol, 0 g fiber, 129 mg sodium

PITA STUFFED WITH HUMMUS AND VEGGIES

Prep Time: 10 minutes; Cook Time: none; Total Time: 10 minutes

Serve with chilled melon for a light meal.

  2 whole wheat pitas (6" diameter), toasted
  4 tablespoons prepared roasted garlic hummus
  4 tablespoons fat-free plain yogurt
  1/4 teaspoon dried oregano
      Ground black pepper
  1/2 small seedless cucumber, peeled and chopped
  1/2 small red onion, thinly sliced
  1/4 cup crumbled reduced-fat feta cheese
  4 lettuce or spinach leaves, shredded
      Sliced bottled or fresh hot peppers (optional)

Cut the pitas in half and open carefully. Spread 1 tablespoon each of the hummus and yogurt into each pocket. Season lightly with the oregano and black pepper. Stuff with the cucumber, onion, cheese, lettuce or spinach, and hot peppers, if using.

MAKES 4 SERVINGS

PER SERVING: 142 calories, 7 g protein, 23 g carbohydrates, 3 g fat (1 g saturated), 4 mg cholesterol, 4 g fiber, 360 mg sodium

TOTAL FITNESS GUIDE 2009

W|H

TUNA-RICE PAPER WRAP

Prep Time: 10 minutes; Cook Time: none; Total Time: 10 minutes;

Rice-paper wrappers make this recipe different and fun.

- 1 can (12 ounces) water-packed light tuna, drained
- 2 tablespoons reduced-fat mayonnaise
- 1 tablespoon chopped scallion
- 1 tablespoon chopped celery
- 1 tablespoon finely shredded carrot
- 1 tablespoon finely chopped cilantro, plus additional for garnish
- 1/2 teaspoon toasted sesame oil
- Pinch of salt
- Pinch of ground black pepper
- Hot-pepper sauce (optional)
- 4 round rice-paper wrappers

In a bowl, combine the tuna, mayonnaise, scallion, celery, carrot, cilantro, oil, salt, pepper, and a few drops of hot-pepper sauce (if using). Stir to mix well.

Prepare the rice-paper wrappers according to the package directions. Lay the papers on a moistened tray or work surface. Spoon one-fourth of the tuna mixture on one side of each wrapper. Roll up from the bottom, folding sides in first, into a tube. Garnish with cilantro leaves and serve immediately.

MAKES 4 SERVINGS

PER SERVING: 120 calories, 20 g protein, 2 g carbohydrates, 3 g fat (0.5g saturated), 23 mg cholesterol, 0 g fiber, 371 mg sodium

CALIFORNIA SPECIAL

Prep Time: 5 minutes; Cook Time: none; Total Time: 5 minutes

Serve with a chunky vegetable soup.

- 4 slices multigrain bread, toasted
- 1 tablespoon stone-ground mustard
- 2 slices red onion, $\frac{1}{4}$" thick
- 1 ripe avocado, sliced
- 2 slices tomato, $\frac{1}{4}$" thick
- 2 slices ($1\frac{1}{2}$ ounces) Monterey Jack cheese
- 1 cup alfalfa sprouts

Lay 2 slices of the bread on a work surface. Spread with the mustard. Separate the onion slices and distribute on the bread. Top with the avocado, tomato, cheese, sprouts, and remaining bread slices. Cut each sandwich diagonally.

MAKES 4 SERVINGS

PER SERVING: 204 calories, 8 g protein, 20 g carbohydrates, 11 g fat (3 g saturated), 10 mg cholesterol, 8 g fiber, 208 mg sodium

INDIAN POTATO FLATBREAD

Prep Time: 15 minutes; Cook Time: 45 minutes; Total Time: 60 minutes

Low in calories and high on flavor, this savory flatbread makes a delicious and healthful meal.

- 1 pound russet potatoes, peeled and cut into chunks
- 2 serrano or other green chile peppers, cut into pieces (Wear plastic gloves when handling.)
- 1 teaspoon salt
- 2 tablespoons chopped cilantro
- 1 teaspoon garam masala
- 1 cup whole wheat flour

In a saucepan, combine the potatoes, peppers, and $1/2$ teaspoon of the salt. Add enough water to cover. Cover the pan and set over high heat. Bring to a boil. Reduce the heat to medium. Cook for about 20 minutes, or until the potatoes are very tender. Drain. Add the cilantro and garam masala and mash with a potato ricer or masher. Set aside for about 10 minutes to cool to room temperature.

In a mixing bowl, combine the potato mixture with the flour and remaining $1/2$ teaspoon salt. Stir, adding 1 tablespoon of water at a time, to make a moist but not sticky dough. Turn onto a lightly floured work surface. Knead lightly for about 30 seconds, or until the dough forms a smooth ball. Cover with a cloth and let stand for 10 minutes.

Lightly dust your hands with flour. Divide the ball into 12 pieces. With your palms, shape each piece into a ball. Cover the dough while working with one ball at a time. With a rolling pin on a work surface lightly dusted with flour, roll a ball into a 6" circle. Dust lightly with flour; set aside. Continue rolling until all the breads are ready.

Lightly coat a stove-top griddle or other heavy skillet with cooking spray and set over medium-high heat. Place several breads in a single layer on the griddle. Cook for about $1^1/_2$ minutes, or until brown spots form on the bottom. Turn over and cook for about 1 minute longer, or until cooked through. Remove. Continue until all the breads are cooked. Serve immediately.

MAKES 12 SERVINGS

PER SERVING: 67 calories, 2 g protein, 15 g carbohydrates, 0 g fat , 0 mg cholesterol, 2 g fiber, 198 mg sodium

GUILT-FREE ALFREDO PIZZA

Prep Time: 10 minutes; Cook Time: 10 minutes; Total Time: 20 minutes

This unusual pizza is bound to get your tastebuds' attention.

- 2 teaspoons olive oil
- 1 teaspoon minced garlic
- 1 bag (6 ounces) fresh baby spinach
- 4 low-fat flour tortillas (7" diameter)
- 3 tablespoons grated Parmesan cheese
- 1 can (5–6 ounces) white chicken meat, drained
- 3 slices turkey bacon, cooked and crumbled
- ¾ cup (3 ounces) shredded mozzarella cheese

Preheat the oven to 400°F.

In a nonstick skillet over low heat, warm the oil and garlic for about 1 minute, or until the garlic sizzles. Add the spinach. Cook, tossing, for about 2 minutes, or until wilted.

Set the tortillas in a single layer on a baking sheet. Sprinkle each with the Parmesan. Cover with an even layer of the spinach and chicken. Top with the bacon. Sprinkle the mozzarella on top. Bake for 7 to 10 minutes, or until the cheese is bubbly. Cut each pizza into wedges.

MAKES 4 SERVINGS

PER SERVING: 285 calories, 18 g protein, 24 g carbohydrates, 13 g fat (4.5 g saturated), 39 mg cholesterol, 5 g fiber, 773 mg sodium

HAWAIIAN MUFFIN PIZZA

Prep Time: 10 minutes; Cook Time: 12 minutes; Total Time: 22 minutes

Delicious, fast, and easy!

- 3 English muffins, split and lightly toasted
- 4 ounces reduced-fat ham, cut into small cubes
- 1 green bell pepper, chopped
- 1 cup pineapple tidbits in juice, drained, or finely chopped fresh pineapple
- 4 ounces shredded reduced-fat sharp Cheddar cheese

Preheat the oven to 375°F.

Set the muffins, cut side up, on a baking sheet. Top with the ham, pepper, pineapple, and cheese. Bake for 12 minutes, or until the cheese is bubbly.

MAKES 6 SERVINGS

PER SERVING: 164 calories, 11 g protein, 18 g carbohydrates, 5 g fat (3 g saturated), 19 mg cholesterol, 1 g fiber, 504 mg sodium

YES PIZZAS

Prep Time: 5 minutes; Cook Time: 15 minutes; Total Time: 20 minutes

Served with a yummy fresh salad, this pizza is so filling and pleasing that no one feels deprived.

2 teaspoons olive oil

8 ounces mushrooms, sliced

1 cup grape tomatoes, sliced

½ teaspoon dried oregano

Pinch of salt

Pinch of ground black pepper

4 low-fat tortillas (7" diameter)

⅓ cup pizza sauce

½ cup (2 ounces) shredded part-skim mozzarella cheese

Red-pepper flakes (optional)

MAKES 4 SERVINGS

PER SERVING: 199 calories, 8 g protein, 24 g carbohydrates, 8 g fat (1 g saturated), 0 mg cholesterol, 5 g fiber, 408 mg sodium

Preheat the oven to 400°F.

In a nonstick skillet over medium-high heat, warm the oil. Add the mushrooms. Toss. Cover and cook, tossing occasionally, for about 4 minutes, or until liquid pools in the pan. Uncover and cook for about 2 minutes longer, or until the liquid is gone. Add the tomatoes, oregano, salt, and pepper. Remove from the heat.

Lay the tortillas on a large baking sheet. With the back of a spoon, spread the sauce evenly over the tortillas. Evenly sprinkle on half of the cheese. Top evenly with the mushroom mixture and the remaining cheese. Bake for about 8 minutes, or until the cheese is bubbly. Sprinkle with the red-pepper flakes, if desired.

SUMMER SQUASH PARMIGIANA

Prep Time: 10 minutes; Cook Time: 20 minutes; Total Time: 30 minutes

This is a great recipe for shedding pounds because it is quick and easy, and it easily sneaks vegetables and dairy into your diet.

- 1 can (14½ ounces) tomato sauce
- 2 teaspoons dried Italian seasoning
- 1 clove garlic, minced
- ¼ teaspoon salt
- ¼ teaspoon ground black pepper
- 3 small yellow squash or zucchini, unpeeled, cut into 1" chunks
- 3 tablespoons seasoned dry bread crumbs
- ¼ cup grated Parmesan cheese
- ½ cup shredded part-skim mozzarella cheese

Coat a 2-quart microwaveable gratin dish or other shallow baking dish with cooking spray.

In a bowl, combine the tomato sauce, seasoning, garlic, salt, and pepper. Spread a few tablespoons of the sauce on the bottom of the prepared dish. Cover with a layer of the squash. Repeat with 2 more layers of sauce and squash, ending with the remaining sauce. Sprinkle with the bread crumbs, Parmesan, and mozzarella.

Microwave on high power for about 18 minutes, or until the squash is cooked and the cheese is bubbly.

MAKES 6 SERVINGS

PER SERVING: 86 calories, 6 g protein, 10 g carbohydrates, 3 g fat (1.5 g saturated), 9 mg cholesterol, 2 g fiber, 606 mg sodium

GRILLED STUFFED EGGPLANT

Prep Time: 15 minutes; Cook Time: 25 minutes; Total Time: 40 minutes

A filling yet healthful meal.

  3 small eggplants, halved lengthwise
  ¼ cup grated Parmesan cheese
  ¼ cup seasoned dry bread crumbs
  3 plum tomatoes, finely chopped
  1 tablespoon chopped fresh parsley
  4 cloves garlic, minced
  ¼ teaspoon salt
  ¼ teaspoon ground black pepper
  2 tablespoons olive oil

Preheat a covered grill to medium-high.

With a small, sharp knife, cut a grid of ½" squares on the cut side of each eggplant half, as close to the skin as possible without cutting through. Scoop out the flesh of each eggplant and place in a medium bowl. Add the cheese, bread crumbs, tomatoes, parsley, garlic, salt, and pepper. Stir to mix. Stuff the mixture tightly into each eggplant half. Drizzle with the oil.

Place the eggplant halves in a disposable aluminum foil pan. Set on the grill. Cover and grill for 20 to 25 minutes, or until the eggplant is soft and the top is golden and crisp.

MAKES 6 SERVINGS

PER SERVING: 150 calories, 5 g protein, 21 g carbohydrates, 7 g fat (1.5 g saturated), 3 mg cholesterol, 10 g fiber, 244 mg sodium

SQUASH AND CORN DELIGHT

Prep Time: 15 minutes; Cook Time: 10 minutes; Total Time: 25 minutes

This delicious medley of veggies gives the old peas-and-carrots combo a run for its money.

 1 tablespoon canola oil

 1 small onion, finely chopped

 4 medium yellow squash or zucchini or a
    combination, unpeeled, cubed
    Kernels cut from 2 ears of corn (about
    1¾ cups)

 1 jalapeño chile pepper, chopped (wear
    plastic gloves when handling)

 ½ teaspoon salt

In a large skillet over medium heat, warm the oil. Add the onion. Cook, stirring occasionally, for about 2 minutes, or until the onion begins to soften. Add the squash. Turn the heat to high. Cook, stirring frequently, for about 6 minutes, or until softened and golden. Add the corn, chile pepper, and salt. Cook for about 2 minutes, or until the corn is heated through.

MAKES 4 SERVINGS

PER SERVING: 115 calories, 5 g protein, 16 g carbohydrates, 5 g fat (0.5 g saturated), 0 mg cholesterol, 4 g fiber, 303 mg sodium

GREEN BEANS WITH DILL

Prep Time: 10 minutes; Cook Time: 5 minutes; Total Time: 15 minutes

Aromatic fresh dill really makes this dish. Fresh basil is also good if you don't have dill.

- 1 pound green beans, cut into 2" lengths
- 2 teaspoons butter or trans fat–free margarine
- ½ cup chopped red onion
- 1 tablespoon finely chopped fresh dill or 1 teaspoon dried dill
- ¼ teaspoon salt
- ¼ teaspoon ground black pepper

Boil or steam the beans until tender but still crisp. Drain and set aside.

In a nonstick skillet over medium heat, melt the butter or margarine. Add the onion. Cook, stirring occasionally, for about 3 minutes, or until slightly softened. Add the reserved beans, the dill, salt, and pepper. Toss for about 2 minutes, or until the flavors combine.

MAKES 4 SERVINGS

PER SERVING: 53 calories, 2 g protein, 9 g carbohydrates, 2 g fat (1 g saturated), 5 mg cholesterol, 5 g fiber, 160 mg sodium

TOMATOES STUFFED WITH WHITE BEAN SALAD

Prep Time: 15 minutes; Cook Time: none; Total Time: 15 minutes;

This makes a great lunch-box treat or light supper. It can also be a substantial side dish with grilled fish.

- 2 tablespoons chopped fresh Italian parsley, chopped, plus several sprigs for garnish
- 1 tablespoon lemon juice
- 1 tablespoon extra-virgin olive oil
- 2 teaspoons capers, rinsed and drained
- 2 cloves garlic, minced
- 1/4 teaspoon salt
- 1/4 teaspoon freshly ground black pepper
- 1 can (15 1/2 ounces) navy beans, drained and rinsed
- 4 medium tomatoes

In medium bowl, combine the parsley, lemon juice, oil, capers, garlic, salt, and pepper. Whisk to mix. Add the beans. Toss thoroughly to mix. For a slightly creamier texture, mash one-quarter of the beans roughly with the back of a fork.

Slice 1/4" from the tops of the tomatoes. Scoop out the seeds and discard. Spoon the bean salad into the tomatoes. Garnish with parsley sprigs.

MAKES 4 SERVINGS

PER SERVING: 155 calories, 8 g protein, 24 g carbohydrates, 4 g fat (0.5 g saturated), 0 mg cholesterol, 6 g fiber, 572 mg sodium

ALL-PURPOSE SKILLET VEGGIES

Prep Time: 20 minutes; Cook Time: 15 minutes; Total Time: 35 minutes;

You can serve this as a meal, a side dish, or a filling for anything! It's particularly good on large tortillas with some mozzarella cheese and a little green chile sauce.

- 1 tablespoon olive oil
- 1 bell pepper, any color, chopped
- ½ sweet onion, chopped
- 4 garlic cloves, thinly sliced
- 1 medium zucchini, chopped
- 1 medium yellow squash, chopped
- 1 large tomato, chopped
- 2 tablespoons chopped fresh parsley
- ½ teaspoon dried oregano
- ½ teaspoon dried basil
- ¼ teaspoon salt
- ¼ teaspoon ground black pepper

In a large nonstick skillet over medium heat, warm the oil. Add the bell pepper, onion, and garlic. Cook, stirring occasionally, for about 4 minutes, or until starting to soften. Add the zucchini and squash. Turn the heat to high. Cook, stirring frequently, for about 6 minutes, or until the squash starts to turn golden. Add the tomato. Cook, stirring, for about 3 minutes, or until the tomato softens. Add the parsley, oregano, basil, salt, and pepper. Cook for 1 minute for the seasonings to blend.

MAKES 4 SERVINGS

PER SERVING: 80 calories, 3 g protein, 11 g carbohydrates, 4 g fat (0.5 g saturated), 0 mg cholesterol, 3 g fiber, 160 mg sodium

VEGAN SESAME GRILL

Prep Time: 10 minutes; Cook Time: 25 minutes; Total Time: 35 minutes

The brilliant flavor of these grilled vegetables is so satisfying!

- 2 sweet potatoes, peeled and cut into walnut-size chunks
- 8 ounces Brussels sprouts, halved
- 4 garlic cloves, thinly sliced
- 2 teaspoons canola oil
- ¼ teaspoon salt
- ½ teaspoon regular or hot toasted sesame oil
  Freshly ground black pepper

Preheat a covered grill.

In a large bowl, combine the sweet potatoes, Brussels sprouts, garlic, canola oil, and salt. Toss to coat. Place the vegetables in a grill basket or portable grill rack. Set on the grill and cover. Grill, turning occasionally, for 20 to 25 minutes, or until tender. Transfer the vegetables to a platter. Drizzle the sesame oil on top. Season to taste with black pepper. Toss.

MAKES 4 SERVINGS

PER SERVING: 154 calories, 4 g protein, 23 g carbohydrates, 5 g fat (0.5 g saturated), 0 mg cholesterol, 4 g fiber, 183 mg sodium

KALE WITH PUMPKIN SEEDS

Prep Time: 10 minutes, plus standing; Cook Time: 5 minutes; Total Time: 15 minutes

Filling, nutritious, low-calorie, and simply delicious as a side or main dish..

- $1/2$ teaspoon plus $1/8$ teaspoon salt
- 1 pound kale leaves, coarsely chopped
- 1 tablespoon canola oil
- 2 teaspoons rice vinegar, plus additional for serving
- 1 tablespoon toasted pumpkin seeds

In a pot, combine $1/2$ teaspoon salt and the kale in enough water to cover. Let stand for 30 minutes. Drain the kale, leaving any water clinging to leaves.

In the same pot over medium-high heat, warm the oil. Add the kale and cook, tossing occasionally, for about 5 minutes, or until wilted. Add the vinegar and the remaining $1/8$ teaspoon salt. Toss. Serve sprinkled with the seeds. Pass additional vinegar at the table.

MAKES 4 SERVINGS

PER SERVING: 92 calories, 4 g protein, 12 g carbohydrates, 5 g fat (0.5 g saturated), 0 mg cholesterol, 2 g fiber, 340 mg sodium

CARROT AND PINEAPPLE-ORANGE GELATIN MOLD

Prep Time: 15 minutes, plus chilling; Cook Time: none; Total Time: 15 minutes

Junk snacking is a downfall for many of us. You can satisfy many different cravings with this gelatin recipe.

- 1 large package (6 ounces) orange gelatin
- 2 cups boiling water
- ¼ cup pineapple juice
- 2 cups grated carrots
- 1½ cups reduced-fat small-curd cottage cheese
- 1 cup crushed unsweetened pineapple, drained
- ½ cup light mayonnaise
- ¼ cup slivered almonds

Coat a 9" × 13" glass or ceramic dish with cooking spray.

In a large bowl, combine the gelatin, water, and juice. Stir until the gelatin is dissolved. Refrigerate for 1 hour, or until slightly congealed.

With a hand-held electric beater or whisk, beat the gelatin mixture until frothy. Add the carrots, cottage cheese, pineapple, mayonnaise, and almonds. Fold to combine. Transfer to the prepared dish. Cover and refrigerate for 1 hour, or until set.

MAKES 12 SERVINGS

PER SERVING: 122 calories, 6 g protein, 20 g carbohydrates, 3 g fat (0.5 g saturated), 1 mg cholesterol, 1 g fiber, 267 mg sodium

GARLIC-LEMON POTATOES

Prep Time: 10 minutes; Cook Time: 15 minutes; Total Time: 25 minutes

They're healthy and very flavorful!

- 1½ pounds red-skin or yellow potatoes, cubed
- ½ teaspoon salt
- 2 tablespoons lemon juice
- 1 tablespoon olive oil
- 2 cloves garlic, minced
  Freshly ground black pepper

In a saucepan, combine the potatoes and salt with enough water to cover by 1". Cook over medium heat for about 15 minutes, or until tender. Drain and return to the pan. Add the lemon juice, oil, garlic, and pepper to taste. Toss to mix thoroughly.

MAKES 6 SERVINGS

PER SERVING: 102 calories, 2 g protein, 19 g carbohydrates, 2 g fat (0.5 g saturated), 0 mg cholesterol, 2 g fiber, 201 mg sodium

INSTANT RICE PILAF

Prep Time: 5 minutes; Cook Time: 20 minutes; Total Time: 25 minutes

Get fiber and nutrients from instant brown rice in a fraction of the time that it takes regular brown rice to cook.

- 2 teaspoons butter or trans fat–free margarine
- 2 tablespoons chopped onion or scallion
- 1 teaspoon salt-free seasoning blend
- ½ teaspoon salt
- 1 cup instant brown rice
- 1 can (14½ ounces) reduced-sodium chicken broth or water
- 1 tablespoon chopped fresh parsley or chives

In a saucepan over medium heat, melt the butter or margarine. Add the onion or scallion, seasoning, and salt. Cook, stirring, for about 2 minutes, or until the onion is sizzling. Add the rice. Stir to coat. Add the broth or water. Bring to a boil. Reduce the heat to a simmer and cover. Cook for 10 minutes. Remove from the heat and set aside for 5 minutes. Fluff with a fork, sprinkle with the parsley or chives, and serve.

MAKES 4 SERVINGS

PER SERVING: 111 calories, 4 g protein, 18 g carbohydrates, 3 g fat (1 g saturated), 5 mg cholesterol, 1 g fiber, 407 mg sodium

TASTY AND COLORFUL QUINOA

Prep Time: 15 minutes; Cook Time: 25 minutes; Total Time: 40 minutes

Replace buttered potatoes or buttered white rice with this cholesterol-cutting side.

- 1½ tablespoons extra-virgin olive oil
- ½ cup chopped red bell pepper
- ½ cup chopped yellow onion
- ½ cup chopped celery
- ½ teaspoon adobo seasoning
- ¼ teaspoon salt
- 1 cup quinoa
- 2 cups reduced-sodium fat-free chicken broth
- ½ cup fresh or frozen corn kernels
- 2 scallions, thinly sliced

In a saucepan over medium heat, warm 1 tablespoon of the oil. Add the bell pepper, onion, celery, seasoning, and salt. Cook, stirring frequently, for 4 minutes, or until the pepper starts to soften. Add the quinoa. Stir to coat. Add the broth and corn. Bring to a boil and cover, then reduce the heat to low. Simmer for 20 minutes, or until all the liquid is absorbed. Stir in the remaining ½ tablespoon oil. Sprinkle with the scallions.

MAKES 4 SERVINGS

PER SERVING: 243 calories, 7 g protein, 37 g carbohydrates, 8 g fat (1 g saturated), 0 mg cholesterol, 4 g fiber, 567 mg sodium

CELEBRATION RICE

Prep Time: 5 minutes; Cook Time: 55 minutes; Total Time: 60 minutes

This side dish combines crunchy roasted sesame seeds and wild rice with lively spices and a hint of citrus.

- ¾ cup Uncle Ben's Natural Whole Grain Brown Rice
- ¼ cup wild rice
- 2 cups water
- ⅓ cup orange juice
- 1 tablespoon reduced-sodium soy sauce
- 1½ teaspoons olive oil
- 1 teaspoon grated orange rind
- 1 teaspoon curry powder
- ½ teaspoon salt
- 2 tablespoons chopped fresh chives or scallions
- 2 tablespoons chopped red bell pepper
- 1 tablespoon toasted sesame seeds

In a 2-quart saucepan over medium heat, stir the brown rice and wild rice for 5 minutes, or until lightly toasted. Add the water, orange juice, soy sauce, oil, orange rind, curry powder, and salt. Cover the pan tightly and cook over low heat for 45 to 50 minutes, or until all the liquid has been absorbed and the rice is tender.

Fluff the rice with a fork. Stir in the chopped chives or scallions, bell pepper, and sesame seeds.

MAKES 4 SERVINGS

PER SERVING: 209 calories, 5 g protein, 38 g carbohydrates, 4 g fat (0.5 g saturated), 0 mg cholesterol, 2 g fiber, 449 mg sodium

RIGATONI WITH SUMMER SQUASH AND MUSHROOMS

Prep Time: 10 minutes; Cook Time: 10 minutes; Total Time: 20 minutes

Very simple, healthy, quick—and delicious!

- 8 ounces rigatoni pasta
- 2 tablespoons olive oil
- 1 medium yellow or green summer squash, halved lengthwise and sliced (about 2 cups)
- 1 cup sliced mushrooms (8–10 mushrooms)
- 1/2 cup sliced carrot
- 1/2 cup sliced scallions, all parts (about 6 scallions)
- 2 tablespoons chopped fresh dill
- 1/2 teaspoon crushed red-pepper flakes
- 1/4 teaspoon salt
- 1/2 cup (2 ounces) shredded reduced-fat Swiss cheese

Cook the pasta according to the package directions. Scoop out 1/2 cup pasta-cooking water and reserve. Drain the pasta and return to the cooking pot to keep warm.

Meanwhile, in a large nonstick skillet over medium-high heat, warm the oil. Add the squash, mushrooms, and carrot. Toss to mix. Cover and cook, stirring occasionally, for 3 to 4 minutes, or until tender-crisp. Add the scallions. Cook for about 2 minutes, or until the carrots are tender and the scallions are wilted. Add the dill, pepper flakes, and salt. Remove from the heat.

Add the pasta to the vegetable mixture. Moisten with a few tablespoons of the reserved cooking water. Add the cheese. Toss over low heat for about 1 minute, or until the cheese melts. Serve warm or at room temperature.

MAKES 4 SERVINGS

PER SERVING: 326 calories, 13 g protein, 48 g carbohydrates, 9 g fat (1.5 g saturated), 5 mg cholesterol, 3 g fiber, 200 mg sodium

SMOTHERED BEAN BURRITOS

Prep Time: 10 minutes; Cook Time: 25 minutes; Total Time: 35 minutes

Beans, a true power food, are an excellent source of low-fat protein and fiber.

   2   teaspoons canola or olive oil
 $\frac{1}{2}$ cup chopped onion
 $\frac{1}{2}$ cup chopped red or yellow bell pepper
   1   tablespoon chili powder
   1   can (16 ounces) fat-free refried beans
   4   whole wheat or regular flour tortillas
       (8" diameter)
   1   can (14$\frac{1}{2}$ ounces) diced tomatoes
   2   jalapeño chile peppers, finely chopped
       (wear plastic gloves when handling)
   1   cup (4 ounces) shredded reduced-fat
       Cheddar cheese

Preheat the oven to 350°F. Coat a 13" × 9" baking dish with cooking spray.

In a small nonstick skillet over medium heat, warm the oil. Add the onion, bell pepper, and chili powder. Cook, stirring occasionally, for about 4 minutes, or until the onion is softened. Set aside half (about $\frac{1}{4}$ cup) of the mixture in a bowl. Add the beans to the skillet and break them up with a spoon. Add a few tablespoonfuls of water, if needed, to loosen the mixture slightly.

Lay the tortillas in a single layer on a work surface. Spoon one-quarter (about $\frac{1}{2}$ cup) of the bean mixture on each tortilla, then fold opposite sides of each tortilla to meet in the middle. Fold the top and bottom of the roll to form a compact bundle. Place the burritos seam side down in the prepared dish.

Add the tomatoes (with juice) and the chile peppers to the reserved onion and pepper mixture. Stir to mix. Spread over the burritos. Sprinkle the cheese on top.

Bake for about 18 minutes, or until the cheese melts and the mixture bubbles.

MAKES 4 SERVINGS

PER SERVING: 329 calories, 16 g protein, 42 g carbohydrates, 11 g fat (4 g saturated), 20 mg cholesterol, 8 g fiber, 1,165 mg sodium

BLACK-BEAN VEGETABLE NOODLE STIR-FRY

Prep Time: 15 minutes; Cook Time: 10 minutes; Total Time: 25 minutes

Easy, delicious, and filling, this dish is low in carbohydrates yet full of vibrant flavor.

- 2 teaspoons olive oil
- 1 medium red bell pepper, chopped
- 1 medium green bell pepper, chopped
- 1 small onion, chopped (about ½ cup)
- 1 small zucchini, halved and cut into chunks
- 2 cloves garlic, minced
- 1 bag (16 ounces) shirataki noodles, drained and rinsed in hot water
- 1 cup canned black beans, drained and rinsed (about half of a 15-ounce can)
- 2 tablespoons reduced-sodium soy sauce
- 1½ teaspoons sodium-free seasoning mix
- 2 tablespoons chopped fresh cilantro or parsley
   Hot-pepper sauce

In a wok or large nonstick skillet over high heat, warm the oil. Add the bell peppers, onion, zucchini, and garlic. Reduce the heat to medium-high and cook, stirring frequently, for 4 minutes, or until the vegetables start to soften. Add the noodles, beans, soy sauce, and seasoning mix. Reduce the heat to medium. Cook, stirring frequently, for 3 to 4 minutes longer, or until the mixture is hot. Add the cilantro or parsley. Toss to mix. Pass the hot-pepper sauce at the table.

MAKES 4 SERVINGS

PER SERVING: 107 calories, 5 g protein, 18 g carbohydrates, 3 g fat (0.5 g saturated), 0 mg cholesterol, 5 g fiber, 539 mg sodium

BOW TIE PASTA WITH SPINACH, TOMATO, AND OLIVES

Prep Time: 10 minutes; Cook Time: 10 minutes; Total Time: 20 minutes

With appealing Mediterranean flavorings, you'll feel like you're vacationing, not watching your waistline. For a nonvegetarian variation, toss in some grilled shrimp or chicken breast.

12 ounces bow tie pasta

2 tablespoons olive oil

2 cloves garlic, finely chopped

2 cups chopped fresh or canned tomatoes

2 cups packed (2 ounces) baby spinach leaves, roughly chopped

2 tablespoons lemon juice, preferably freshly squeezed

2 tablespoons sliced kalamata or other ripe olives

2 tablespoons capers, drained and rinsed

$\frac{1}{4}$ teaspoon ground black pepper

$\frac{1}{8}$ teaspoon salt

2 tablespoons grated Parmesan cheese

Cook the pasta according to the package directions. Before draining, scoop out $\frac{1}{2}$ cup of the pasta-cooking water and reserve. Drain the pasta and return it to the cooking pot to keep warm.

Meanwhile, in a large, nonstick skillet over medium-low heat, combine the oil and garlic. Cook for about 2 minutes, or until the garlic is soft and fragrant. Do not brown. Add the tomatoes and cook for about 4 minutes longer, or until the tomatoes start to soften. Add the spinach and cook, tossing, for about 1 minute more, or until wilted. Stir in the lemon juice, olives, capers, pepper, and salt. Reduce the heat to low.

Add the tomato mixture to the reserved pasta and toss to coat. Add a few tablespoons of the reserved cooking water, if needed, to moisten the pasta. Serve sprinkled with cheese.

MAKES 4 SERVINGS

PER SERVING: 420 calories, g 14 protein, 70 g carbohydrates, 10 g fat (2 g saturated), 2 mg cholesterol, 5 g fiber, 343 mg sodium

VEGETARIAN CABBAGE "LASAGNA"

Prep Time: 20 minutes; Cook Time: 45 minutes; Total Time: 65 minutes

This tasty, protein-packed lasagna layers savory sautéed vegetables and tofu between leaves of tender cabbage. No one will know there's tofu in it!

- 1 head (1½ pounds) green cabbage, cored
- 1 tablespoon olive oil
- ½ cup finely chopped onion
- 1 pound sliced mushrooms
- 6 ounces baby spinach leaves, cut into slices (about 8 cups loosely packed)
- 1 tablespoon Italian seasoning blend
- 1 package (12–14 ounces) silken tofu, drained
- 2 large eggs, beaten
- ¼ cup (1 ounce) grated Parmesan/Romano cheese blend
- ½ teaspoon ground black pepper
- ¼ teaspoon salt
- ¼ teaspoon ground nutmeg
- 1 jar (26 ounces) marinara sauce
- 1 cup (4 ounces) shredded part-skim mozzarella cheese

Separate 12 cabbage leaves from the cabbage and wash in cold water. Reserve the remaining cabbage in the refrigerator for another use. Place 4 to 6 leaves in a resealable plastic storage bag. Microwave on high power for 3 to 4 minutes, rotating, until wilted. Using oven mitts, remove and set aside. Fill another bag with leaves. Microwave until wilted. Empty the first bag; fill it with leaves and microwave. Continue until all the leaves are steamed.

Preheat the oven to 350°F. Coat a 13" × 9" pan with cooking spray.

In a large nonstick skillet over medium-high heat, warm the oil. Add the onion and mushrooms. Toss to coat. Cover and cook for about 5 minutes, or until the liquid pools in the pan. Uncover and cook for about 4 minutes longer, or until the liquid has evaporated. Add the spinach and seasoning. Cook, stirring, for about 2 minutes, or until the spinach is wilted.

In a bowl, combine the tofu, eggs, Parmesan/Romano, pepper, salt, and nutmeg. Stir to blend completely. Coat the bottom of the prepared pan with ¼ cup of the marinara sauce. Line the pan with 4 of the cabbage leaves. Top with half of the tofu mixture, half of the mushroom mixture, and about ⅔ cup sauce. Cover with 4 of the cabbage leaves. Top with the remaining tofu mixture, mushroom mixture, and ⅔ cup sauce. Cover with the remaining leaves and sauce. Sprinkle the mozzarella on top. Bake for about 30 minutes, or until bubbly and the cheese is golden.

MAKES 6 SERVINGS

PER SERVING: 263 calories, 18 g protein, 23 g carbohydrates, 12 g fat (4 g saturated), 88 mg cholesterol, 7 g fiber, 979 mg sodium

BROWN RICE DOLMADES

Prep Time: 40 minutes; Cook Time: 45 minutes; Total Time: 85 minutes

You can prepare these tasty stuffed bundles in advance, then reheat individual portions in the microwave.

  1 cup brown rice (about 3 cups cooked rice)
 36 drained, preserved grape leaves (5–6 ounces), well rinsed
  2 tablespoons olive oil
  1 cup chopped sweet onion
 ¼ cup tomato sauce
 ¼ cup raisins
 ¼ cup chopped fresh parsley
 ½ teaspoon dried oregano
    Pinch of ground allspice
  1 teaspoon salt
 ½ teaspoon ground black pepper
  1 lemon, thinly sliced
  1 cup water

Prepare the rice according to the package directions.

Rinse the grape leaves well under cold running water. Place in a large bowl and cover with boiling water. Set aside for 10 minutes. Drain and rinse the leaves again in cold water. Set aside.

In a large nonstick skillet over medium-high heat, warm the oil. Add the onion. Cook, stirring often, for about 8 minutes, or until golden. Add the rice, tomato sauce, raisins, parsley, oregano, allspice, salt, and pepper. Reduce the heat to low. Cook, stirring, for about 5 minutes longer. Remove from the heat. Let stand to cool slightly.

Coat a large pot with cooking spray. Scatter a few lemon slices over the bottom of the pot.

Open several grape leaves at a time and lay them, vein side up, on a work surface. Spoon about 1 tablespoon of the filling in the center. Fold the stem end over the filling, then the two sides toward the middle. Roll into a tight tube. Place the stuffed leaves seam side down in the prepared pot. Continue filling, rolling, and packing the leaves into the pan until all the leaves are used. Place the remaining lemon slices on top. Place a heavy heat-proof plate over the leaves to prevent them from floating. Add the water.

Cover and simmer over medium-low heat for about 30 minutes, or until tender.

MAKES 6 SERVINGS

PER SERVING: 194 calories, 4 g protein, 33 g carbohydrates, 6 g fat (1 g saturated), 0 mg cholesterol, 3 g fiber, 1,124 mg sodium

ZESTY EGGPLANT STEW

Prep Time: 15 minutes; Cook Time: 45 minutes; Total Time: 60 minutes

This satisfying dish is packed with healthy veggies, plus a lot of flavor for very few calories.

    1 tablespoon olive oil
    1 medium eggplant, peeled and chopped
    1 medium green bell pepper, chopped
    1 medium onion, chopped (about 1 cup)
    2 cloves garlic, finely chopped
    1 tablespoon chili powder
    1 teaspoon paprika
  $\frac{1}{2}$ teaspoon ground black pepper
  $\frac{1}{4}$ teaspoon salt
    1 tablespoon flour
    2 cans (14$\frac{1}{2}$ ounces each) diced tomatoes
    1 can (15 ounces) tomato sauce
    1 can (15$\frac{1}{2}$ ounces) kidney or pinto beans,
       drained and rinsed
  $\frac{1}{3}$ cup chopped fresh cilantro or parsley
       leaves
  $\frac{1}{4}$ cup grated Parmesan/Romano cheese
       blend

In a large, deep nonstick skillet over medium-high heat, warm the oil. Add the eggplant, bell pepper, onion, garlic, chili powder, paprika, black pepper, and salt. Cook, stirring, for about 5 minutes, or until the vegetables start to soften.

Sprinkle the flour over the mixture. Stir to mix. Add the tomatoes, tomato sauce, and beans. Stir to mix. Reduce the heat to low. Simmer for about 40 minutes, or until the vegetables are tender and the flavors are blended. Stir in the cilantro or parsley.

Serve garnished with the cheese.

MAKES 6 SERVINGS

PER SERVING: 183 calories, 9 g protein, 27 g carbohydrates, 4 g fat (1.5 g saturated), 5 mg cholesterol, 10 g fiber, 872 mg sodium

BLACK BEANS AND CORN WITH RICE

Prep Time: 10 minutes; Cook Time: 15 minutes; Total Time: 25 minutes

Simple but vibrant, this dish comes together in a snap.

2 cups instant or regular brown rice (6 cups cooked)

2 teaspoons olive or canola oil

$\frac{1}{2}$ cup finely chopped onion

1 cup finely chopped red bell pepper

1 teaspoon dried oregano

$\frac{1}{2}$ teaspoon ground cumin

$\frac{1}{8}$ teaspoon ground red pepper

$\frac{1}{4}$ teaspoon salt

$\frac{1}{4}$ teaspoon ground black pepper

1 can ($15\frac{1}{2}$ ounces) black beans, rinsed and drained

1 cup sweet white corn kernels

1 cup vegetable broth or water

1 teaspoon grated lime peel

$\frac{1}{4}$ cup freshly squeezed lime juice

PER SERVING: 264 calories, 11 g protein, 49 g carbohydrates, 3 g fat (0.5 g saturated), 0 mg cholesterol, 9 g fiber, 629 mg sodium

Prepare the rice according to the package directions.

Meanwhile, in a large nonstick skillet over medium heat, warm the oil. Add the onion, bell pepper, oregano, cumin, ground red pepper, salt, and black pepper. Cook, stirring, for about 5 minutes, or until the vegetables are starting to soften. Add the beans and corn and stir until blended. Add the broth or water. Reduce the heat to low. Simmer for about 10 minutes.

With a fork, stir the rice into the bean mixture. Add the lime peel and juice. Toss to mix well.

MAKES 6 SERVINGS

VEGETARIAN CURRY BURGERS

Prep Time: 15 minutes; Cook Time: 20 minutes; Total Time: 35 minutes

Enjoy these spicy burgers on toasted wheat buns with Simple Slaw (page 318) on the side.

2	tablespoons olive or canola oil
1	medium onion, chopped
1	teaspoon curry powder
1/2	teaspoon ground coriander
1/2	teaspoon crushed fennel seeds
1 1/2	cups white button mushrooms, chopped
1 1/2	cups drained cooked chickpeas
1	medium carrot, grated
1/4	cup chopped walnuts
3	tablespoons chopped cilantro
1/2	teaspoon salt
1/4	teaspoon ground black pepper
	Flour

In a medium nonstick skillet over medium high heat, warm 1 tablespoon of the oil. Add the onion, curry powder, coriander, and fennel seeds. Cook, stirring frequently, for about 2 minutes, or until the onion starts to soften. Add the mushrooms. Stir to mix. Cover and cook for about 4 minutes longer, or until the liquid pools in the pan. Uncover and cook for about 3 minutes more, or until the liquid is evaporated.

Transfer the mixture to the bowl of a food processor fitted with a metal blade. Add the chickpeas. Pulse until well chopped. Transfer to a bowl. Add the carrot, walnuts, cilantro, salt, and pepper and mix well.

Lightly dust hands with flour. Shape the mixture into six 4"-wide patties. In a large skillet over medium heat, warm the remaining 1 tablespoon oil. Place the patties in the pan. Cook for about 4 minutes, or until browned on the bottom. Flip and cook for about 4 minutes longer, or until heated through.

MAKES 6 SERVINGS

PER SERVING: 169 calories, 6 g protein, 18 g carbohydrates, 9 g fat (1 g saturated), 0 mg cholesterol, 5 g fiber, 18 mg sodium

VEGETABLE FAJITAS

Prep Time: 15 minutes; Cook Time: 5 minutes; Total Time: 20 minutes

It's the colorful vegetables and exciting seasonings that make fajitas so appealing!

- 2 tablespoons olive oil
- 1 large onion, halved and sliced
- 1 red bell pepper, cut into strips
- 1 yellow bell pepper, cut into strips
- 1 green bell pepper, cut into strips
- 8 ounces mushrooms, stems removed, sliced
- 1 tablespoon chili powder
- 2 cloves garlic, minced
- ¼ teaspoon salt
- ⅛ teaspoon ground black pepper
- 4 whole wheat tortillas (8" diameter)
- 1 small ripe avocado, sliced
- ½ cup grape tomatoes, sliced (about 12 tomatoes)
- ¼ cup chopped fresh cilantro plus optional sprigs for garnish

PER SERVING: 297 calories, 6 g protein, 34 g carbohydrates, 17 g fat (2 g saturated), 0 mg cholesterol, 9 g fiber, 389 mg sodium

In a large nonstick skillet over high heat, warm the oil for 1 minute. Add the onion, bell peppers, mushrooms, chili powder, garlic, salt, and black pepper. Cook, tossing frequently, for about 6 minutes, or until the vegetables are just tender.

Meanwhile, heat the tortillas according to the package directions.

Spoon the vegetable mixture onto the tortillas. Top with avocado, tomatoes, and cilantro. Roll up and serve garnished with cilantro sprigs, if desired.

MAKES 4 SERVINGS

ORANGE COCONUT SHRIMP

Prep Time: 15 minutes, plus standing; Cook Time: 20 minutes; Total Time: 35 minutes

Even indulgence foods like coconut are okay on a weight-loss diet. Just keep moderation in mind.

Dip

- ½ cup low-sugar or artificially sweetened orange marmalade
- 2 tablespoons spicy brown mustard
- 1 tablespoon lime juice, preferably freshly squeezed

Shrimp

- ½ cup rice wine vinegar
- 2 tablespoons olive oil
- 2 teaspoons minced garlic
- ¼ teaspoon red-pepper flakes
- ¼ teaspoon salt
- ⅛ teaspoon ground black pepper
- 1 pound jumbo shrimp, peeled, deveined, and rinsed
- ½ cup unsweetened flaked coconut
- ¼ cup low-sugar or artificially sweetened orange marmalade

Preheat the oven to 350°F.

To prepare the dip: In a saucepan, combine the marmalade, mustard, and lime juice. Cook, stirring constantly, over medium heat, for about 4 minutes, or until the mixture bubbles. Remove from the heat. Let stand to cool.

To prepare the shrimp: In a mixing bowl, combine the vinegar, oil, garlic, pepper flakes, salt, and black pepper. Whisk to mix. Add the shrimp. Toss to coat. Let stand for 15 minutes to marinate.

Meanwhile, scatter the coconut in a thin layer over a baking sheet. Bake, stirring occasionally, for about 7 minutes, or until lightly browned. Remove and let stand to cool.

Coat a stove-top griddle or baking sheet with cooking spray. Preheat the griddle or the broiler. Drain the shrimp and discard the marinade. Thread 4 or 5 shrimp on each of 4 metal or soaked bamboo skewers. Cook for about 3 minutes per side, or until no longer opaque. Remove the shrimp to a tray. Brush both sides of the shrimp with the marmalade.

Sprinkle on the coconut, pressing lightly to adhere. Serve with the dip.

MAKES 4 SERVINGS

PER SERVING: 329 calories, 21 g protein, 23 g carbohydrates, 16 g fat (7.5 g saturated), 151 mg cholesterol, 1 g fiber, 395 mg sodium

ROASTED ORANGE TILAPIA AND ASPARAGUS

Prep Time: 5 minutes; Cook Time: 20 minutes; Total Time: 25 minutes

Roasting asparagus in the oven really concentrates the flavor and retains the nutrients. Any mild white-fleshed fish can take the place of the tilapia.

- ¼ cup orange juice
- 1½ tablespoons olive oil
- 2 teaspoons minced garlic
- 1½ teaspoons herbes des Provence
- ¼ teaspoon salt
- ¼ teaspoon ground black pepper
- 1 pound tilapia fillets
- 12 ounces asparagus, trimmed
   Orange slices

Preheat the oven to 375°F. Coat a 13" × 9" baking dish with cooking spray. Add the orange juice, oil, garlic, herbes de Provence, salt, and pepper. Stir to mix. Place the fish in the pan.

Cut the asparagus into 1½"-long pieces. Place in the pan around the fish. Flip the fish twice and stir the asparagus to thoroughly coat with the orange mixture.

Bake, stirring the asparagus once or twice, for 15 to 20 minutes, or until the fish flakes easily with a fork. Serve garnished with orange slices and drizzled with the pan juices.

MAKES 4 SERVINGS

PER SERVING: 190 calories, 25 g protein, 6 g carbohydrates, 7 g fat (1.5 g saturated), 57 mg cholesterol, 2 g fiber, 326 mg sodium

GRECIAN SCALLOP SALAD

Prep Time: 10 minutes; Cook Time: 5 minutes; Total Time: 15 minutes

Try this light main dish for a summer meal with fresh fruit on the side.

Salad

- 16 medium sea scallops
- 2 tablespoons lemon juice
- 2 teaspoons minced garlic
- 1 teaspoon water
- 3 cups chopped romaine lettuce
- 2 medium tomatoes, chopped
- 1 medium cucumber, chopped
- 1 cup cooked rice
- 1 cup crushed tomatoes
- ¼ cup diced onion
- 2 tablespoons crumbled reduced-fat feta cheese

Dressing

- ¼ cup red wine vinegar
- 1½ tablespoons balsamic vinegar
- 1 tablespoon olive oil
- 1½ tablespoons minced fresh parsley
- 1 tablespoon dried basil
- 1 teaspoon garlic powder
- 1 teaspoon hot-pepper sauce (optional)
- ¼ teaspoon dried oregano
- ⅛ teaspoon ground black pepper

To prepare the salad: Coat a large nonstick skillet with cooking spray. Over medium heat, cook the scallops for 4 minutes. Add the lemon juice, garlic, and water. Cook for 2 to 3 minutes longer, or until the scallops are opaque. Set aside to cool.

In a large bowl, toss together the lettuce, chopped tomatoes, and cucumber. Cover with the rice, crushed tomatoes, onion, and reserved scallops. Sprinkle with the cheese.

To prepare the dressing: In a large bowl, combine the red wine vinegar, balsamic vinegar, oil, parsley, basil, garlic powder, hot-pepper sauce (if using), oregano, and black pepper. Whisk. Pour over the salad and toss well.

MAKES 4 SERVINGS

PER SERVING: 217 calories, 16 g protein, 28 g carbohydrates, 5 g fat (1 g saturated), 22 mg cholesterol, 5 g fiber, 281 mg sodium

SHRIMP IN GREEN TEA-CURRY SAUCE

Prep Time: 10 minutes; Cook Time: 10 minutes; Total Time: 20 minutes

This dish is so simple to prepare, yet it's sophisticated enough to share with guests. The delicate tea flavor is delightfully enhanced by the subtle curry.

  8 ounces linguine
  1 cup boiling water
  1 tablespoon green tea leaves
  1 tablespoon canola oil
  1 pound large shrimp, peeled, deveined, and rinsed
  ¼ cup finely chopped scallions, white and light green parts
  2 teaspoons minced garlic
  1½ teaspoons hot or mild curry powder
  2 tablespoons sake or dry white wine
  1 teaspoon toasted sesame oil
     Chopped cilantro and sliced scallions

Cook the linguine according to the package directions, subtracting 2 minutes of the cooking time. Drain and return to the cooking pot to keep warm.

In a heatproof container, combine the boiling water and tea. Cover and steep for 5 minutes.

Meanwhile, heat the canola oil in a large nonstick skillet or wok over high heat. Add the shrimp, chopped scallions, garlic, and curry powder. Cook, tossing, for 1 minute. Add the sake or wine. Cook for 30 seconds. Add the tea and half of the tea leaves. Cook for 1 minute, or until the shrimp are opaque. With a slotted spoon, remove the shrimp and set aside.

Transfer the linguine to the skillet or wok. Reduce the heat to medium-low. Cook, tossing, for about 3 minutes, or until the linguine is al dente and the sauce has thickened. Return the shrimp to the pan. Drizzle with the sesame oil. Toss to combine. Garnish with the cilantro and sliced scallions.

MAKES 6 SERVINGS

PER SERVING: 260 calories, 21 g protein, 30 g carbohydrates, 5 g fat (0.5 g saturated), 115 mg cholesterol, 2 g fiber, 115 mg sodium

CHICKEN A LA PROSCIUTTO

Prep Time: 15 minutes; Cook Time: 25 minutes; Total Time: 40 minutes

This chicken main dish is elegant enough for a special occasion yet remarkably low in calories.

4	boneless, skinless chicken breasts (1¼ pounds)
¼	cup flour
1	tablespoon butter
1	tablespoon extra-virgin olive oil
8	ounces mushrooms, sliced
¾	cup dry white wine
¾	cup chicken broth
¼	teaspoon salt
½	teaspoon ground black pepper
4	slices prosciutto ham
4	slices (2 ounces) thinly sliced provolone cheese
2	tablespoons chopped fresh parsley

Place the chicken on a work surface. Cover with plastic wrap. Pound to ½" thickness. Dust both sides of the chicken lightly with the flour. Shake off the excess.

In a large nonstick skillet over high heat, warm the butter and oil. In two batches, cook the chicken for about 3 minutes on each side, or until no longer pink and the juices run clear. Remove to a plate. Set aside.

Set the same skillet over medium-high heat. Add the mushrooms and toss. Cover and cook, stirring occasionally, for about 4 minutes, or until the mushrooms give off liquid. Uncover and cook for 2 minutes longer, or until the liquid evaporates. Add the wine. Cook for about 3 minutes, or until the liquid evaporates. Add the broth, salt, and pepper. Bring to a simmer. Return the reserved chicken to the pan. Reduce the heat to medium-low. Top with the prosciutto and cheese. Cover and cook for about 2 minutes, or until the cheese is melted.

Place the chicken on a platter. Top with the mushrooms and sauce. Sprinkle with the parsley.

MAKES 4 SERVINGS

PER SERVING: 368 calories, 43 g protein, 9 g carbohydrates, 14 g fat (5.5 g saturated), 111 mg cholesterol, 1 g fiber, 836 mg sodium

CURRIED CHICKEN AND BROCCOLI CASSEROLE

Prep Time: 10 minutes; Cook Time: 50 minutes; Total Time: 60 minutes

It's a cinch to assemble this oven-baked dinner up to a day ahead of cooking. Simply cool the broccoli before putting all the ingredients together. Cover with plastic wrap and refrigerate until baking time.

1 pound broccoli florets

¼ cup water

1 can (10¾ ounces) reduced-sodium cream of mushroom soup

¼ cup mayonnaise

1 tablespoon lemon juice

1½ teaspoons curry powder

½ teaspoon salt

½ teaspoon ground black pepper

1½ pounds boneless, skinless chicken breasts, cut into bite-size chunks

¼ cup shredded reduced-fat Colby or Swiss cheese

PER SERVING: 255 calories, 30 g protein, 9 g carbohydrates, 11 g fat (2.5 g saturated), 73 mg cholesterol, 3 g fiber, 571 mg sodium

Preheat the oven to 350°F. Coat a 13" × 9" baking dish with cooking spray.

Place the broccoli and water in a large resealable plastic storage bag. Microwave on high power, rotating occasionally, for 3 to 5 minutes, or until bright green. Drain and set aside.

In a small bowl, mix the soup, mayonnaise, lemon juice, curry powder, salt, and pepper. Stir to mix. Line the prepared baking dish with the reserved broccoli. Top with the chicken. Cover evenly with the soup mixture. Sprinkle with the cheese. Cover and bake for about 25 minutes. Uncover and bake for 15 to 20 minutes longer, or until golden and bubbling.

MAKES 6 SERVINGS

CHICKEN, CORN, AND TOMATILLO CHILI

Prep Time: 15 minutes; Cook Time: 25 minutes; Total Time: 40 minutes

If you can afford a few extra calories, top each serving with 2 teaspoons shredded reduced-fat Cheddar cheese and 2 teaspoons mashed avocado or light sour cream.

- 1 tablespoon olive or canola oil
- 1 large onion, chopped
- 3 cloves garlic, minced
- 1 teaspoon ground cumin
- 1 teaspoon chili powder
- ½ teaspoon dried oregano
- ½ teaspoon ground coriander
- ¼ teaspoon salt
- ¼ teaspoon ground black pepper
- 12 ounces boneless, skinless chicken breasts, cut into cubes
- 2 cans (14½ ounces each) fat-free reduced-sodium chicken broth
- 1 can (14½ ounces) salt-free diced tomatoes
- 1 can (4 ounces) tomatillos, drained and chopped
- 1 can (4 ounces) chopped green chiles, drained
- 1 package (10 ounces) frozen corn kernels, thawed
- 1 can (15 ounces) white beans or pinto beans, drained and rinsed
- 1 lime, cut into wedges
  Chopped cilantro

In a large, deep nonstick skillet over medium heat, warm the oil. Add the onion, garlic, cumin, chili powder, oregano, coriander, salt, and black pepper. Cook, stirring occasionally, for 3 to 5 minutes, or until the onion has softened. Add the chicken and continue cooking for 5 minutes longer, or until the chicken is browned. Add the broth, tomatoes (with juice), tomatillos, and chiles. Bring to a boil. Reduce the heat. Simmer, stirring occasionally, for 10 minutes, allowing the flavors to blend. Add the corn and beans. Cook, stirring occasionally, for 5 minutes longer.

Serve with lime and cilantro.

MAKES 8 SERVINGS

PER SERVING: 161 calories, 15 g protein, 19 g carbohydrates, 3 g fat (0.5 g saturated), 25 mg cholesterol, 4 g fiber, 516 mg sodium

EZ TRIM FAJITAS

Prep Time: 15 minutes; Cook Time: 10 minutes; Total Time: 25 minutes

This satisfying dish is full of color and bursts of fresh flavors. Use this recipe a few times a week, but change up the veggies or spices. Try garam masala instead of the cumin.

1 tablespoon canola oil

1 pound boneless, skinless chicken breasts, cut into strips

½ green bell pepper, cut into strips

½ cup red bell pepper, cut into strips

½ small red onion, sliced

2 teaspoons ground cumin

¼ teaspoon salt

¼ teaspoon ground black pepper

½ cup bottled or homemade salsa

1 jalapeño chile pepper, chopped or sliced (wear plastic gloves when handling)

12 whole wheat tortillas (7" diameter), heated

6 lime wedges

Shredded lettuce

1 tomato, sliced

Sliced scallions (optional)

Sliced cucumber (optional)

Shredded reduced-fat Cheddar cheese (optional)

Fat-free sour cream (optional)

In a large nonstick skillet over medium heat, warm the oil. Add the chicken. Cook, stirring occasionally, for about 5 minutes, or until lightly browned.

Add the bell peppers, onion, cumin, salt, and black pepper. Cook, tossing frequently, for about 4 minutes longer, or until the bell peppers are crisp-tender. Add the salsa and chile pepper.

Cook for 1 minute more, or until heated through. Test that the juices from the chicken run clear and no pink remains.

Serve with the tortillas, lime, lettuce, and tomato. Garnish each serving with scallions, cucumber, cheese, and sour cream, if desired.

MAKES 6 SERVINGS

PER SERVING: 333 calories, 22 g protein, 39 g carbohydrates, 9 g fat (0.5 g saturated), 44 mg cholesterol, 7 g fiber, 685 mg sodium

MEXICALI CHICKEN BAKE

Prep Time: 15 minutes; Cook Time: 1 hour, 10 minutes; Total Time: 1 hour, 25 minutes

Serve this robust dish with Spanish rice or with tortillas, fajita-style.

- 1 tablespoon olive or canola oil
- 1 onion, cut into rings
- 1 green bell pepper, cut into strips
- 1 tablespoon chili powder
- 1 clove garlic, minced
- ¼ teaspoon salt
- 2 cups tomato puree
- 1 cup canned vegetarian refried beans
- ½ cup low-fat sour cream (optional)
- 1 jalapeño chile pepper, finely chopped (optional; wear plastic gloves when handling)
- 1 pound boneless, skinless chicken breasts, sliced crosswise
- ¾ cup shredded reduced-fat Colby Jack cheese
- Finely chopped cilantro (optional)

Preheat the oven to 350°F. Coat a 13" × 9" baking dish with cooking spray.

In a medium nonstick skillet over medium heat, warm the oil. Add the onion, bell pepper, chili powder, garlic, and salt. Stir to mix. Cover the skillet and cook, stirring occasionally, for 5 minutes, or until softened. Add the tomato puree, beans, sour cream (if using), and chile pepper (if using). Stir to mix. Simmer for about 3 minutes, or until heated through.

Place the chicken in the prepared dish. Cover with the sauce. Sprinkle the cheese on top. Cover with foil and bake for 1 hour, or until a thermometer inserted in the thickest portion of the chicken registers 160°F and the juices run clear. Remove the foil. If desired, broil 6" from the heat source for about 2 minutes or until the cheese is bubbly. Top with cilantro, if desired.

MAKES 6 SERVINGS

PER SERVING: 249 calories, 25 g protein, 18 g carbohydrates, 9 g fat (3.5 g saturated), 59 mg cholesterol, 4 g fiber, 806 mg sodium

LEMON CHICKEN OREGANO

Prep Time: minutes; 5 Cook Time: 15 minutes; Total Time: 20 minutes

Bake this chicken just until it's no longer pink in the center and you'll be rewarded with a juicy, succulent supper.

- 2 boneless, skinless chicken breasts (6 ounces each)
- 2 tablespoons lemon juice
- 1 tablespoon butter or trans fat–free margarine, melted
- 3/4 teaspoon dried oregano
- 1/2 teaspoon lemon pepper seasoning
- 1/8 teaspoon salt
- 2 teaspoons finely chopped fresh parsley or chives (optional)

Preheat the oven to 375°F. Coat a small baking dish with cooking spray.

Place the chicken in a single layer in the prepared dish. Pour the lemon juice and butter or margarine over the chicken. Sprinkle with the oregano, lemon pepper, and salt. Bake for about 15 minutes, or until a thermometer inserted in the thickest portion registers 160°F and the juices run clear. Serve drizzled with the pan juices. Sprinkle with the parsley or chives, if using.

MAKES 2 SERVINGS

PER SERVING: 204 calories, 33 g protein, 2 g carbohydrates, 7 g fat (2 g saturated), 82 mg cholesterol, 0 g fiber, 313 mg sodium

TURKEY, BLACK BEAN, AND BEER CHILI

Prep Time: 20 minutes; Cook Time: 2 hours, 15 minutes; Total Time: 2 hours, 35 minutes

This recipe is high in protein and complex carbohydrates but low in fat. It is extremely satisfying (the flavor is sufficiently complex to energize all the tastebuds) and fills you up. Serve over high-protein pasta if you're craving pasta as well.

2	tablespoons extra-virgin olive oil
1	medium yellow onion, chopped
1	small yellow bell pepper, chopped
1	small orange bell pepper, chopped
1	rib celery, chopped)
1	carrot, chopped
3	cloves garlic, minced
2	teaspoons chili powder
2	teaspoons dried oregano
1	teaspoon ground cumin
1/2	teaspoon salt
1 1/2	pounds lean ground turkey breast
4	cups chopped fresh plum tomatoes or canned plum tomatoes with juice
3	cups cooked black beans
1	bottle (12 ounces) light beer
1/2	teaspoon ground black pepper

In a large, deep nonstick skillet set over medium-high heat, warm the oil. Add the onion, bell peppers, celery, carrot, garlic, chili powder, oregano, cumin, and salt. Stir. Cover and cook, stirring occasionally, for about 10 minutes, or until the peppers are softened.

Crumble the turkey into the skillet. Cook, breaking up the turkey with the back of a spoon, for about 5 minutes, or until no longer pink. Add the tomatoes, beans, and beer. Bring to a boil, then reduce the heat to a simmer. Cover the skillet and simmer for 1 hour, stirring occasionally to prevent sticking. Remove the cover and continue simmering, stirring occasionally, for 1 hour.

MAKES 6 SERVINGS

PER SERVING: 224 calories, 30 g protein, 11 g carbohydrates, 7 g fat (1 g saturated), 45 mg cholesterol, 3 g fiber, 283 mg sodium

WINTER CHILI

Prep Time: 15 minutes; Cook Time: 1 hour, 10 minutes; Total Time: 1 hour, 25 minutes;

Ground sirloin is a great alternative to ground chuck. The other ingredients in this heart-warming chili contain lots of protein and vitamins without the high fat of some chili recipes.

    1   tablespoon canola oil
    1   medium onion, chopped
    1   green bell pepper, chopped
    3   cloves garlic, minced
    1   pound ground top sirloin beef
 1½   tablespoons mild or hot chili powder
 1½   teaspoons ground cumin
   ½   teaspoon salt
    1   can (28 ounces) tomato puree
    1   can (28 ounces) petite diced tomatoes
    2   cans (15½ ounces each) dark red kidney
        beans, drained and rinsed
        Chopped cilantro
        Shredded reduced-fat sharp Cheddar
        cheese (optional)

In a large, deep nonstick skillet over medium-high heat, warm the oil. Add the onion, pepper, and garlic. Stir to mix. Cover the skillet. Cook for about 4 minutes, or until the onions and pepper start to soften. Scrape to one side of the skillet.

Crumble the beef into the skillet. Cook, stirring, for about 5 minutes, or until no longer pink. Add the chili powder, cumin, and salt. Cook, stirring, for 1 minute longer, or until the spices are fragrant. Add the tomato puree, tomatoes (with juice), and beans. Stir to mix. Reduce the heat to medium-low. Partially cover the skillet. Cook, stirring occasionally, for about 1 hour, or until the flavors are well blended. Sprinkle each serving with the cilantro and cheese, if using.

MAKES 6 SERVINGS

PER SERVING: 332 calories, 28 g protein, 41 g carbohydrates, 7 g fat (1.5 g saturated), 36 mg cholesterol, 13 g fiber, 586 mg sodium

TURKEY SAUSAGE AND PEPPERS

Prep Time: 15 minutes; Cook Time: 1 hour, 15 minutes; Total Time: 1 hour, 30 minutes

With its leaner protein and lots of veggies, this is good traditional comfort food that is good for you. It's a perfect recipe to have on hand for parties, so all your family stays healthy!

2 tablespoons olive oil

1 large red bell pepper, cut into thin strips

1 large green bell pepper, cut into thin strips

2 medium yellow onions, cut into thin strips

3 cloves garlic, finely chopped

1 pound mild or hot Italian turkey sausage, cut into 4 equal pieces

1 can (28 ounces) crushed tomatoes in thick puree

1 teaspoon dried Italian seasoning

1 teaspoon crushed red-pepper flakes (optional)

Pinch of salt

PER SERVING: 356 calories, 24 g protein, 26 g carbohydrates, 20 g fat (1 g saturated), 68 mg cholesterol, 6 g fiber, 997 mg sodium

In a large, deep nonstick skillet over medium heat, warm the oil. Add the bell peppers, onions, and garlic. Cook, stirring frequently, for about 10 minutes, or until the peppers are softened. Remove the vegetables to a bowl.

Add the sausage to the same skillet. Cook, turning as needed, for 5 to 6 minutes, or until browned on all sides. Add the reserved pepper-and-onion mixture, tomatoes, seasoning, pepper flakes (if using), and salt. Bring to a boil, then reduce to a simmer. Simmer for about 1 hour, or until the sausage is fork-tender.

MAKES 4 SERVINGS

PORK KEBABS ITALIANO

Prep Time: 20 minutes; Cook Time: 10 minutes; Total Time: 30 minutes

Robust Romano cheese and dried Italian herbs are all it takes to liven up lean pork tenderloin and healthy veggies. These kebabs are good enough for a party.

- ¼ cup dry bread crumbs
- 2 tablespoons grated Pecorino Romano cheese
- 2 teaspoons Italian seasoning
- 2 teaspoons minced garlic
- ½ teaspoon salt
- ¼ teaspoon ground black pepper
- 12 ounces boneless pork loin, cut into 1" cubes
- ½ carton (5 ounces) grape or cherry tomatoes (about 1 cup)
- 1½ cups frozen pearl onions, thawed
- 1 tablespoon olive oil

MAKES 4 SERVINGS

PER SERVING: 292 calories, 24 g protein, 28 g carbohydrates, 10 g fat (3 g saturated), 57 mg cholesterol, 5 g fiber, 467 mg sodium

Preheat a grill.

In a small bowl, combine the bread crumbs, cheese, seasoning, garlic, salt, and pepper. Toss to mix. Set aside.

In a medium bowl, combine the meat, tomatoes, and onions. Toss with the oil to coat. Thread the meat, tomatoes, and onions alternately on 8 metal or soaked bamboo skewers, putting an even number of ingredients on each skewer. Place on a tray. Sprinkle with the bread crumb mixture, making sure that all surfaces are coated evenly.

Grill the skewers, turning often, for about 10 minutes, or until the pork is no longer pink and the juices run clear.

PEACHY OAT BREAKFAST

Prep Time: 4 minutes; Cook Time: 2 minutes; Total Time: 6 minutes

When peaches are not in season, use thawed frozen peaches or drained canned or jarred peaches in juice.

- 1 cup water
- ¼ cup oat bran
- 2 tablespoons protein powder
- 1 teaspoon sugar
- ½ cup chopped fresh peaches
  Ground cinnamon

In a microwaveable bowl, combine the water, oat bran, protein powder, and sugar. Stir to mix well. Microwave on high power for about 2 minutes, checking every 30 seconds, or until thickened and the liquid is absorbed. Stir in the peaches and sprinkle with cinnamon to taste.

MAKES 1 SERVING

PER SERVING: 214 calories, 25 g protein, 32 g carbohydrates, 3 g fat (1 g saturated), 13 mg cholesterol, 5 g fiber, 44 mg sodium

YOGURT-AND-BRAN BREAKFAST FEAST

Prep Time: 4 minutes; Cook Time: none; Total Time: 4 minutes

This recipe contains a lot of fiber, so it is low in calories but filling—and it cleanses your system.

- $\frac{1}{2}$ cup low-fat vanilla yogurt
- $\frac{1}{3}$ cup Fiber One cereal
- $\frac{1}{2}$ banana, sliced

In a serving bowl, combine the yogurt, cereal, and banana. Stir gently to mix.

MAKES 1 SERVING

PER SERVING: 197 calories, 8 g protein, 47 g carbohydrates, 2 g fat (1 g saturated), 6 mg cholesterol, 11 g fiber, 151 mg sodium

YOGURT-AND-BRAN BREAKFAST FEAST

Prep Time: 4 minutes; Cook Time: none; Total Time: 4 minutes

This recipe contains a lot of fiber, so it is low in calories but filling—and it cleanses your system.

- ¹/₂ cup low-fat vanilla yogurt
- ¹/₃ cup Fiber One cereal
- ¹/₂ banana, sliced

In a serving bowl, combine the yogurt, cereal, and banana. Stir gently to mix.

MAKES 1 SERVING

PER SERVING: 197 calories, 8 g protein, 47 g carbohydrates, 2 g fat (1 g saturated), 6 mg cholesterol, 11 g fiber, 151 mg sodium

OMELET ITALIAN-STYLE

Prep Time: 5 minutes; Cook Time: 10 minutes; Total Time: 15 minutes

If you have some fresh basil leaves on hand, cut them into slivers and toss into the omelet with the tomatoes.

- 1 tablespoon chopped onion
- 1 tablespoon chopped green bell pepper
- 1 tablespoon chopped tomato, plus additional for garnish
- 1 egg, beaten
- 2 egg whites, beaten
- 1/2 teaspoon Italian seasoning
- 1 teaspoon grated Parmesan cheese

In a medium nonstick skillet coated with cooking spray over medium heat, add the onion and pepper. Cook, stirring occasionally, for about 2 minutes, or until sizzling. Add the tomato. Cook for about 1 minute longer, or until just starting to soften. Add the egg and egg whites. Sprinkle with the seasoning. Reduce the heat to low and cook for about 5 minutes, lifting the cooked edges of the egg mixture with a fork so the uncooked egg can run underneath, or until the bottom is set. Cook for 1 to 2 minutes, or until the eggs are cooked through. Sprinkle with the cheese and fold the omelet in half. Garnish with additional chopped tomato.

MAKES 1 SERVING

PER SERVING: 123 calories, 15 g protein, 3 g carbohydrates, 6 g fat (2 g saturated), 213 mg cholesterol, 1 g fiber, 208 mg sodium

CITRUS-AVOCADO SALAD

Prep Time: 10 minutes; Cook Time: none; Total Time: 10 minutes

This salad provides lots of potassium and vitamin C and is a filling lunch.

Salad

- 8 cups mixed salad greens
- 2 navel oranges, separated into segments and chopped
- 1 avocado, chopped
- 1 tablespoon chopped walnuts

Dressing

- 2 tablespoons lime juice
- 2 tablespoons extra-virgin olive oil
- 1 tablespoon finely chopped cilantro
- ¼ teaspoon salt
- ⅛ teaspoon ground red pepper

To prepare the salad: In a large shallow salad bowl, arrange the greens. Top with the oranges and avocado. Sprinkle with the walnuts.

To prepare the dressing: In a small bowl, whisk together the lime juice, oil, cilantro, salt, and pepper. Drizzle over the salad. Toss gently.

MAKES 6 SERVINGS

PER SERVING: 135 calories, 2 g protein, 11 g carbohydrates, 10 g fat (1.5 g saturated), 0 mg cholesterol, 5 g fiber, 119 mg sodium

BROCCOLI SALAD

Prep Time: 5 minutes, plus chilling; Cook Time: none; Total Time: 5 minutes

This is an easy salad to make. It's always a hit, and you get your fresh raw veggies!

- 1 bag (8 ounces) fresh precut broccoli, cut into bite-size pieces
- 2 tablespoons chopped red onion
- ¼ cup light balsamic salad dressing
  Freshly ground black pepper
- 1 tablespoon grated Parmesan/Romano cheese blend

In a large bowl, combine the broccoli and onion. Drizzle the dressing on top. Season to taste with pepper. Toss to mix. Refrigerate for 1 hour to chill. Serve sprinkled with the cheese.

MAKES 6 SERVINGS

PER SERVING: 24 calories, 2 g protein, 4 g carbohydrates, 1 g fat (0.5 g saturated), 1 mg cholesterol, 1 g fiber, 154 mg sodium

SIMPLE SLAW

Prep Time: 15 minutes; Cook Time: none; Total Time: 15 minutes

There's wonderful fiber in these veggies.

- 1 small head (2 pounds) green or red cabbage, thinly sliced (about 14 cups)
- 1 small red onion, thinly sliced
- 6 tablespoons red wine vinegar
- 3 tablespoons extra-virgin olive oil
- $\frac{1}{2}$ teaspoon salt
- Freshly ground black pepper

In a large bowl, combine the cabbage and onion. In a cup, whisk together the vinegar, oil, salt, and pepper to taste. Drizzle the dressing over the salad. Toss to mix well.

MAKES 12 SERVINGS

PER SERVING: 56 calories, 1 g protein, 5 g carbohydrates, 4 g fat (0.5 g saturated), 0 mg cholesterol, 2 g fiber, 115 mg sodium

GREEN BEAN VEGETABLE SALAD

Prep Time: 10 minutes, plus chilling; Cook Time: 1 minute; Total Time: 10 minutes

This recipe is a great side dish that is low in calories. Serve it instead of a green salad, which, over time, can get boring.

- ¼ cup red or white wine vinegar
- 1 tablespoon water
- 2 teaspoons sugar or Splenda
- ⅛ teaspoon salt
- 3 tablespoons canola or olive oil
- 1 package (16 ounces) frozen French-style green beans, thawed
- 1 package (10 ounces) frozen baby peas, thawed
- 1 package (10 ounces) frozen white kernel corn, thawed
- ½ cup chopped onion
- ½ cup chopped celery
- 1 jar (4 ounces) pimientos, drained
- 2 slices turkey bacon, cooked and crumbled

PER SERVING: 161 calories, 6 g protein, 19 g carbohydrates, 8 g fat (1 g saturated), 7 mg cholesterol, 5 g fiber, 276 mg sodium

In a microwaveable bowl, whisk together the vinegar, water, sugar or Splenda, and salt. Cover and microwave on high power for 1 minute or until the sugar or Splenda is dissolved. Set aside to cool to room temperature.

Pour the vinegar mixture into a large bowl. Add the oil and whisk to blend. Add the beans, peas, corn, onion, celery, and pimientos. Toss to mix. Cover and refrigerate, stirring occasionally, for at least 3 hours. Top with the bacon bits before serving.

MAKES 8 SERVINGS

EASY SUMMER CUCUMBER SALAD

Prep Time: 10 minutes; Cook Time: none; Total Time: 10 minutes

This is a tasty side dish with a grilled chicken breast or salmon steak.

- 1 large English cucumber, halved lengthwise
- 1 cup cherry tomatoes, halved
- $1/2$ cup thinly sliced red onion
- $1/3$ cup reduced-fat sour cream
- 2 tablespoons white wine vinegar
- 2 teaspoons sugar or Splenda
- 2 tablespoons chopped olives
- $1/4$ teaspoon salt
  Freshly ground black pepper

Cut the cucumber halves into $1/4$"-thick slices. Transfer to a large bowl. Add the tomatoes, onion, sour cream, vinegar, sugar or Splenda, olives, and salt. Toss to mix. Season to taste with pepper.

MAKES 6 SERVINGS

PER SERVING: 41 calories, 1 g protein, 5 g carbohydrates, 2 g fat (1 g saturated), 5 mg cholesterol, 1 g fiber, 129 mg sodium

CORKSCREW PASTA VEGETABLE SALAD

Prep Time: 20 minutes, plus chilling; Cook Time: 2 minutes; Total Time: 20 minutes

Boost nutrients by tossing crispy vegetables into pasta salad.

Dressing

- 1 cup light mayonnaise or salad dressing
- 1 tablespoon minced fresh dill
- 1 teaspoon minced garlic
- ¼ teaspoon salt

Salad

- 4 cups broccoli florets, cut into bite-size pieces
- 6 ounces corkscrew pasta, cooked, drained, and cooled (about 3 cups)
- 2 small carrots, chopped
- 1 cup cherry or grape tomatoes, each halved
- 6 radishes, sliced
- 1 small red onion, chopped
- 2 tablespoons sliced black olives
- Ground black pepper

MAKES 8 SERVINGS

PER SERVING: 209 calories, 4 g protein, 24 g carbohydrates, 11 g fat (1.5 g saturated), 11 mg cholesterol, g fiber, 357 mg sodium

To prepare the dressing: In a large bowl, combine the mayonnaise or salad dressing, dill, garlic, and salt. Set aside.

To prepare the salad: Place the broccoli in a shallow microwaveable dish in a single layer. Add a few tablespoons of water. Cover and microwave for 2 minutes on high power. Remove and drain.

To the dressing in the bowl, add the broccoli, pasta, carrots, tomatoes, radishes, onion, and olives. Season to taste with pepper. Toss to mix well. Cover and refrigerate for several hours to chill.

LUSCIOUS LIME SHRIMP SALAD

Prep Time: 10 minutes, plus chilling; Cook Time: 3 minutes; Total Time: 15 minutes

Here's a lovely salad, low in calories and carbs, that's perfect any day of the week.

1½ tablespoons lime juice, preferably freshly squeezed

1 tablespoon chopped cilantro

1 small scallion, white and green parts, chopped

1½ teaspoons hoisin sauce

½ teaspoon extra-virgin olive oil

¼ teaspoon minced garlic

Pinch of ground white pepper

8 ounces large shrimp, peeled, deveined, and rinsed

1 tablespoon chopped red bell pepper

Bibb lettuce leaves

PER SERVING: 151 calories, 24 g protein, 5 g carbohydrates, 3 g fat (0.5 g saturated), 173 mg cholesterol, 1 g fiber, 235 mg sodium

In a large bowl, combine the lime juice, cilantro, scallion, hoisin sauce, oil, garlic, and white pepper. Whisk to mix.

In a large nonstick skillet over medium heat, warm 1 tablespoon of the juice mixture. Add the shrimp. Cook, tossing, for 2 to 3 minutes, or until the shrimp are opaque. Pour the skillet contents into the remaining juice mixture in the large bowl. Add the bell pepper. Cover and refrigerate, tossing occasionally, for 30 minutes. Place two serving dishes in the refrigerator, if desired.

Line each chilled plate with lettuce leaves. Spoon the shrimp and some of the marinade onto the lettuce.

MAKES 2 SERVINGS

W|H

FRESH MOZZARELLA SALAD

Prep Time: 10 minutes, plus marinating; Cook Time: none; Total Time: 10 minutes

This is very quick to make and quite filling. You can't beat fresh ingredients.

- 12 ounces fresh mozzarella cheese, drained and sliced
- 6 ripe plum tomatoes, sliced
- 2 tablespoons extra-virgin olive oil
- ½ teaspoon dried oregano
- ⅛ teaspoon salt
  Freshly ground black pepper
- 6 fresh basil leaves, thinly sliced (optional)

In a large shallow dish, arrange the cheese and tomatoes. In a small bowl, combine the oil, oregano, and salt. Whisk to blend. Drizzle over the cheese and tomatoes. Cover and marinate for 1 hour.

Season to taste with pepper and drizzle with the marinating juices. Sprinkle the basil on top, if desired.

MAKES 6 SERVINGS

PER SERVING: 216 calories, 11 g protein, 3 g carbohydrates, 17 g fat (9 g saturated), 41 mg cholesterol, 1 g fiber, 224 mg sodium

credits

index

Underscored page references indicate boxed text.
Boldface references indicate photographs or illustrations.

A

TOTAL FITNESS GUIDE 2009

W|H